NATIVE AMERICANS

NATIVE AMERICANS

Patriotism, Exceptionalism, and the New American Identity

JAMES S. ROBBINS

Encounter Books New York • London

First American edition published in 2013 by Encounter Books, an activity of Encounter for Culture and Education, Inc., a nonprofit, tax exempt corporation.
Encounter Books website address: www.encounterbooks.com

Manufactured in the United States and printed on acid-free paper. The paper used in this publication meets the minimum requirements of ANSI/NISO Z39.48 1992 (R 1997) (*Permanence of Paper*).

FIRST AMERICAN EDITION

LIBRARY OF CONGRESS CATALOGING-IN-PUBLICATION DATA

Robbins, James S., 1962-
Native Americans: patriotism, exceptionalism, and the new American identity/by James S. Robbins.
p. cm.
Includes bibliographical references and index.
ISBN 978-1-59403-610-1 (hardcover: alk. paper)—ISBN 978-1-59403-611-8 (ebook) 1. Indians of North America—Politics and government. 2. Indians of North America—Ethnic identity. 3. Indians of North America—Cultural assimilation. 4. National characteristics, American. 5. United States—Ethnic relations. 6. United States—Politics and government. I. Title.
E98.T77R64 2012
323.1197—dc23

2012015039

CONTENTS

one

INTRODUCTION: THE WAR ON AMERICANS

Are you a native American? I am. I was born here, raised here, and seldom go abroad. I am indigenous to the North American continent, as is my culture. So I have as much right to the title American as anyone else of similar circumstances. Of course, I am not what the United States government defines as a Native American; by that I mean I am not descended from the peoples who populated this continent thousands of years before I showed up. My tribe came much later, not that it matters. I have a right to live here, and the Native Americans have a right to live here, too. We have the same rights—no more, no less.

I don't consider myself a hyphenated American: not a European-American, White-American, Anglo-American, Irish-American, or any other subspecies of American, except maybe suburban-American. The U.S. government describes me as "white non-Hispanic," along with two-thirds of the population. It is a strange non-hyphenated identity, like non-dairy creamer—we know what it isn't, but what exactly is it? But as an American I am free to reject my government classification. My Americanism needs no prefix or suffix.

I am an American by birth, culture, and temperament, but these days what does being an American mean? It does not mean being a citizen of the United States, which is to say it is not a narrow legal definition. People are Americans first, and citizens second. Americans lived on these lands long before there was a country called the United States. People lived here in freedom long before there was a U.S. Constitution and Bill of Rights. The United States is a country; Americans are a people. There are those who are not U.S. citizens who by every meaningful measure could claim the title American. And there are those who have all the benefits of U.S. citizenship who bitterly denounce America and all it stands for.

Opinions differ in the United States over what is means to be part of the American experiment. Some say "American" with pride, others with a sense of guilt or self-consciousness. A few won't say it at all. There are citizens of the United States today who are anything but Americans, a fair portion of whom are embarrassed for and ashamed of their fellow citizens. They feel the need to apologize when referred to as American. They can never say anything positive about their country without immediately saying "but."

American identity is fighting a two-front war, against globalists seeking to dilute it, and multiculturalists trying to carve it up. Globalists believe the American nation is fading and becoming increasingly irrelevant. In the globalist view, ethnic and national divisions are quickly—and fortunately—withering away. Technology has made the world increasingly fluid; global trade, transportation, travel, and communications are more rapid and less expensive than ever. Countries are but lines on a map with no inherent meaning. They are the collections of rule sets competing in the global marketplace, not always fairly, but tending toward a semi-capitalistic ideal. Globalization is a market-driven mechanism, powered by individual needs and desires, in which states can either lead, follow, or get out of the way. In its mature form the globalist view constitutes its own internationalist culture of peace, prosperity, and tolerance. The more "connected" the world becomes, the more it approaches this happy and conflict-free state. National distinctions are meaningless, and to the extent people irrationally cling to them, they slow down the inevitable homogenization of the planet. To globalists, national culture is a marketing gimmick; in their ideal world it would persist chiefly on restaurant menus.

In the globalist world, affinity communities grow through transnational connections based on some category of interest—politics, sports, faith, art, hobbies, or sexuality. These connections can become more important to people than "real life" relationships such as family, neighborhood, or community. "Connecting" is the answer to social alienation, the antidote to the "lonely crowd." The connected world promises self-actualization for all through a combination of growing economies and vibrant social networks. People get what they want, and no one sits in judgment.

In some respects this is a very American outlook. It was invented here and exported from here. Globalization is the Americanizing of the world. It breaks boundaries, awakens aspirations, appeals to the instinct for human freedom. It opens markets and liberates minds. And like any revolutionary force, it disrupts societies, threatens traditions, and alarms the status quo. Those who are most jeopardized by the spread of the American ideal are also most conscious of its true nature. When Osama bin Laden sought to explain why al Qaeda was making war on the United States in his November 2002 "Letter to the American People," he wrote, "I regret to inform you that you are the worst civilization in the history of man." His litany of complaints—against democracy, capitalism, women's rights, freedom of expression, and separation of church and state—were all aimed at quintessential American values. The foundational ideals that Americans take for granted and feel are unquestionable are in fact despised by large segments of the world's population. Critics mocked President George W. Bush for saying that the Islamist terrorists "hate our freedoms," but that is exactly what bin Laden was saying.

While globalists water down the idea of America even as they bring it to the world, multiculturalists have been chopping it up. In their view "American" has no necessary or legitimate meaning outside of a strictly legal definition. Multiculturalists emphasize subnational identities, which they believe are the only ones that are true and meaningful. To them American is defined by otherness, by being part of something apart from the whole, *ex uno plures.*

For multiculturalists there is no unifying American culture, and "American" is not an ethnic group. They define people within groups and cultures that are present in the United States but are not to be thought of primarily, if at all, as American. The oppositional posture of multiculturalism is expressed in politics by exalting the victimhood of the various groups they have identified. They must, by definition, be apart from America, outside of it, and morally superior to it, in order to press claims against it. And anyone who is not identified with a victim group is necessarily part of the oppressor class, guilty from birth and obligated to pay an outstanding debt forever.

In the multiculturalist critique, America is a nightmare culture and the U.S. Constitution is its original sin. It is the land of slavery, Jim Crow, segregation, and racism. It is a country of bigotry and religious persecution. It is a product of the worst excesses of uncaring capitalism, with rampant economic inequality, poverty, and trampled opportunity. It is the country of economic imperialism, of Wall Street and corporate greed. It is a country built on exploitation and subjugation. It is the global hegemon, imperialistic and warlike; engaging in conflict, assassination, covert operations, torture, and coups; ready to terminate any who stand in its path. It is the country of the Red Scare, Japanese internment camps, McCarthyism, My Lai, Watergate, Abu Ghraib, and Guantanamo Bay. Those who dissent from the status quo are harassed by the authorities, their speech chilled, their right to assemble denied, their freedoms sacrificed. Any new outrage becomes a self-evident moral indictment of the system and a new debt owed to the oppressed people. Their hatred of America is boundless.

Given these views it is no surprise that America's civic myths—the things people believe and accept as tokens of legitimacy—are under concerted assault. Whether it is the discovery of the New World ("Columbus destroyed utopia"), the Founding Fathers (white male slave owners), the Constitution (the "dead hand of history"), the westward expansion (Indian genocide), taming the continent (ecocide), the rise of American industry (robber barons and plutocrats), or the international expansion of U.S. power and influence (American imperialism), no aspect of the legitimizing story of the American people has been untouched. While the globalists discard the past in pursuit of the future, the multiculturalists rewrite history to serve as a platform for their endless grievances.

The consequence of this negative view of the country is growing disenchantment and detachment among the young. Professor William Damon of Stanford University has conducted more than a decade of research on perceptions of citizenship among young Americans. He asked them about the meaning of U.S. citizenship and reported typical responses. For example:

> *"We just had [American citizenship] the other day in history. I forget what it was." Another student told us that "being American is not really special. . . . I don't find being an American citizen very important." Another replied, "I don't want to belong to any country. It just feels like you are obligated to this country. I don't like the whole thing of citizen . . . I don't like that whole thing. It's like, citizen, no citizen; it doesn't make sense to me. It's like to be a good citizen—I don't know, I don't want to be a citizen . . . it's stupid to me."*[1]

A free society whose young people have been trained to think the worst of it, or believe that being a citizen is stupid, will not long endure. It is not a house divided, but a tenement with a rotten foundation. In time it will become a standing shell, retaining its facade until suddenly and dramatically collapsing on itself.

"Multiculturalism Has Failed"

The United States is not the only country suffering from multiculturalism's adverse effects. European multiculturalism was a response to a century of nationalist excesses that led to two fratricidal global conflicts and the genocide of the Holocaust. Now Europe's leaders are openly questioning its value.

National consciousness in European states fell into eclipse after the Second World War, but lately has begun to reemerge. In a February 2011 speech, British Prime Minister David Cameron declared the multicultural experiment in Britain "failed." He said that being British meant believing in "freedom of speech and religion, democracy, and equal rights regardless of race, sex, or sexuality." The problem was that for decades the government and society had practiced a "passive tolerance" of immigrant groups that chose not to adopt a British way of life but to remain in their own enclaves, refusing to assimilate into the broader liberal culture. "Under the doctrine of state multiculturalism," Cameron said, "we have encouraged different cultures to live separate lives, apart from each other and the mainstream. We have failed to provide a vision of society to which they feel they want to belong." The result was a growing threat from extremist ideologies that found fertile ground in these culturally isolated communities, particularly among Muslims. He called for Britons actively to promote values of freedom and equality, ensure that all immigrants learn English, and require schools to teach "elements of a common culture and curriculum."[2]

In a speech the following April, Cameron noted that the "woeful welfare system" had created gaps in the labor market exploited by illegal immigrants and temporary workers who come to Britain from outside the European Union, ostensibly for a temporary period, but wind up never leaving. "When there have been significant numbers of new people arriving in neighborhoods," he said, "perhaps not able to speak the same language as those living there, on occasions not really wanting or even willing to integrate, that has created a kind of discomfort and disjointedness in some neighborhoods. . . . This has been the experience for many people in our country and I believe it is untruthful and unfair not to speak about it and address it."[3]

After a series of riots broke out around London in August 2011, British comedian John Cleese said, "London is no longer an English city. That's how they got the Olympics. They said, 'We're the most cosmopolitan city on Earth,' but it doesn't feel English. I had a Californian friend come over two months ago, walk down the King's Road and say to me, 'Well, where are all the English people?' I love having different cultures around but when the parent culture kind of dissipates, you're left thinking, 'What's going on?'"[4] At base, the critics of multiculturalism in Britain are arguing that being British, however it is defined, has inherent value.

Germany's Chancellor Angela Merkel made a similar argument about "multikulti." At "the beginning of the 1960s our country called the foreign workers to come to Germany, and now they live in our country," she said in an October 2010 speech in Potsdam. "We kidded ourselves a while. We said: 'They won't stay, they will be gone,' but this isn't reality. And of course, the approach [to build] a multicultural [society] and to live side-by-side and to enjoy each other . . . has failed, utterly failed."[5]

The Chancellor was echoing German economist and social-democratic politician Thilo Sarrazin's argument in his 2010 best-selling book, *Germany Does Away With Itself.* Sarrazin examined the long-term impact of West Germany's 1961 decision to begin allowing large-scale immigration of Turkish guest workers. The *Gastarbeiter* and their descendants now constitute the largest ethnic minority in Germany, and their demographic profile is young and growing, compared to that of the aging, shrinking ethnic German population. The Turkish immigrants have not assimilated in their host country and, according to Sarrazin, are responsible for "most of the cultural and economic problems" in Germany. "I do not want my grandchildren and great-grandchildren to live in a mostly Muslim country where Turkish and Arabic are widely spoken," he wrote, "women wear headscarves and the day's rhythm is determined by the call of the muezzin."[6] Topics such as this had long been taboo in German politics due to the tragic effects of nationalist extremism under the Nazi regime, culminating in the Holocaust. But Sarrazin's book broke the boundary and became an instant best seller.

French President Nicolas Sarkozy concurred with Mrs. Merkel. In February 2011 he said that multiculturalism in France was "a failure. The truth is that, in all our democracies, we've been too concerned about the identity of the new arrivals and not enough about the identity of the country receiving them." France has Western Europe's largest population of Muslim immigrants, most from North Africa, and has taken the hardest line against accommodating Islamic customs, such as by banning wearing veils in public. "Our Muslim compatriots should be able to live and practice their religion like anyone else," he said, "but it can only be a French Islam and not just an Islam in France."[7]

These comments came in the context of an economic downturn with jobs in short supply, high demand for social services, and government budgets under increasing stress. High unemployment makes it easier for nationalists to scapegoat immigrants. Paradoxically, the tenets of multiculturalism, which emphasize differences, ensure that this will be a continuing political issue. Violent extremists on both sides have exploited the social cleavage. Norwegian terrorist Anders Behring Breivik went on a shooting and bombing rampage in Oslo in July 2011 that left ninety-two people dead. He was motivated by his belief that "there is a core of Cultural Communist elites in Western Europe who really want to destroy Western civilization, European traditions, national solidarity and Christianity."[8] In March 2012, Mohamed Merah, a French citizen of Algerian extraction and self-described member of al Qaeda, killed seven people in a series of three drive-by shootings. The dead included three French paratroopers, a rabbi, and three Jewish schoolchildren. Merah was later killed after a thirty-two-hour standoff with police. Before he was gunned down he boasted that he "brought France to its knees."[9]

But the issue need not inevitably lead to violence. At root is a disagreement over identity and assimilation. The European critics of multiculturalism argue that immigrants to their countries should come only if they desire to assimilate with the culture that defines their nations. Those who want to remain separate, they say, should not bother coming in the first place. This viewpoint asserts that the host cultures are worth maintaining. They are defined by history, language, shared assumptions, values, and civic myths. They are based on all the factors that multiculturalists cite when defending the integrity of every other culture except the predominant one in a given society.

American Nationalism

The question is more complex in the United States, which was built as a nation of immigrants. American nationalism is not based on race, or blood, or land. People become Americans by choice, and each group coming to the United States contributes to the alloy in the "melting pot." But aging America suffers from a hardening of the categories. The ideal of assimilation has given way to a mosaic of affiliations, each of which defines itself and none of which are required or even encouraged to become part of a common American community. Many opinion leaders and politicians believe that America is and should be defined only as a multicultural society in which these divisions are to be preserved, celebrated, and empowered. In this view "diversity" is an unquestioned value, provided it refers only to the approved groups and a limited set of ideas. The country's citizens, to paraphrase President Obama, are required to revere all cultures as they do their own. The old notion of the positive value of abandoning ethnic identity and assimilating into the general culture is denounced as ethnocentric, xenophobic, and, paradoxically, un-American.

Yet not all cultures, beliefs, and practices mesh easily with the Western liberal tradition or the American experience. Humanity is indeed diverse, and it encompasses cultures that condone genital mutilation, dismembering criminals, hanging homosexuals, enforcing strict religious behavior, and condemning women to permanent second-class status. Tolerant America need not tolerate all cultural norms in the pursuit of diversity.

Effectively joining the debate with the multiculturalists requires a root definition of what it means to be an American. It must be grounded in a set of ideals and principles and other factors that define American ethnicity and serve as a baseline for judging the effects of multiculturalism. In short, we need a definition of what "American" means, lest the term refer merely to a legal entity called the United States, a country of increasingly indeterminate culture, rootless constitution, diffident principles, a checkered past, and a haphazard destiny.

The people themselves have provided part of the answer. Since 1980 the Census Bureau has asked an open-ended question about national ancestry. The typical leading responses are German, African, Irish, or English. But growing numbers of people are writing in simply "American." They have cut ties to all other homelands and ethnicities and consider themselves the true product of the American nation. In the multicultural soup of endless categories, divisions, and grievances, they are laying claim to being members of the primary and irreducible culture. That these are write-in responses emphasizes that this is a deliberate choice.

American ethnicity is not a racial category. It is based partly on tradition, and on the central aspects of the American myth: freedom, a sense of destiny, and the American dream. But as importantly, it is based on personal affiliation with a core set of beliefs and a reverence for American values. An immigrant to the United States who is a firm believer in the American ideal can be as much a member of the group as someone with deep family roots in a core "American" region. Likewise, those who reject the defining values of the American experiment are choosing to be outside the group, whether they are from a family that has been in the United States for two months or two hundred years.

Americans are the seekers, the dreamers, the eternal optimists. They are the people on the frontier of human knowledge and experience. They are the proponents of liberty and believers in the American dream. They are the owner-occupiers of the shining city on the hill, the restless idealists who every day transform the world. They are the first new nation, a people self-selected for freedom. They define themselves; they are whoever they want to be. For those unashamed to label themselves as native American—take it, claim it—whether as a birthright, a gift from God, or a self-evident truth. It is yours if you want it.

two

DISCOVERING AMERICA

America's naming was one of history's great misattributions. Genoan explorer Christopher Columbus led the first European Renaissance-era expeditions to the New World in 1492, but it was Amerigo Vespucci of Florence whose name was attached to the continents Columbus had discovered. Vespucci arguably did not achieve enough in his lifetime to have the landmasses of an entire hemisphere named in his honor. But fickle fame often elevates the unworthy, probably more often than not.

To his credit, Vespucci was no mere bystander or popularizer. He undertook several expeditions across the Atlantic in the decade after Columbus' first voyage, and made significant discoveries along what would become the coast of Brazil in service of the king of Portugal. King Ferdinand of Spain installed him as his chief navigator, though his role was chiefly administrative, and afterwards he made no return trips to the New World.

Vespucci's renown in Europe was based on two widely circulated letters he wrote describing his voyages. One of these, Quattuor Americi Vespuccij navigationes (Four Voyages of Americo Vespucci), published in 1504, came to the attention of cartographer

Martin Waldseemüller. He subsequently chose the word "America" to identify the newly discovered lands on his globe and map of the world, Universalis Cosmographia, which was published in 1507. "I do not see what right any one would have to object to calling this part after Americus who discovered it," the accompanying book noted, "and who is a man of intelligence, Amerige, that is, the Land of Americus, or America: since both Europa and Asia got their names from women."[1]

Waldseemüller attached the name "America" to the southern land mass portrayed on his map, a long sliver of what we know as South America, and the area Vespucci actually explored. The northern portion, which represented Central America, the Caribbean, and part of what would become the east coast of the United States, he labeled "Parias," based on a name used by some of the local inhabitants. The name was later omitted, but had it caught on there would be no end of critics of the United States making arch references to the "pariah state" of Parias. It was also fortunate that Waldseemüller did not settle on the more pugnacious "Vespuccia."

Waldseemüller's preemptive naming of America attracted some criticism, and he apparently had second thoughts. In a later edition of the map he abandoned "America" and simply labeled the Western Hemisphere "terra incognita," leaving the official naming to others. But America had already established itself in the European public mind, and the name stuck.

For the next two hundred years "American" was most frequently used in English as an adjective, describing the lands or colonies rather than the people who lived in them. For example, the usage "His Majesty's American Colonies," first seen in the 1640s, simply referred to the geographic location. The word was also used as part of a proper noun to describe animals discovered in the New World, such as the American Martin. When "Americans" was used as a standalone noun it referred to the people who today would be called Native Americans or Indians, not to the European settlers. For example, in 1725 George Berkeley wrote about efforts to bring Christianity to the New World: "It must nevertheless be acknowledged a difficult attempt, to plant religion among the Americans, so long as they continue their wild and roving life. He who is obliged to hunt for his daily food, will have little curiosity or leisure to receive instruction."[2]

The connection of the word "American" to the aboriginal people who lived in the New World also influenced European thinkers who associated the notion of being an American with freedom. And it is certainly possible that in some European quarters referring to the colonists as "Americans" was originally an insult, likening them to the North American "savages." Many people in the United States regard the earliest European settlers as heroic figures, but they were not well respected in their home countries, being seen as a collection of religious fanatics, rough-hewn adventurers, misfits, and malcontents.

By the middle of the eighteenth century, references to "Americans" began to refer to colonists rather than to Indians. An essay published in 1747 discussed the value of sending Protestant missionaries among Indians formerly in the French sphere of influence who had been exposed only to "Popish" clergy. This was necessary, the author argued, both for religious reasons and "to win them over, and firmly attach them to the *English* Interest, an Effect which the *English Americans* know to be highly desirable for their Safety and Advantage."[3] In 1753 an opponent of imposing taxes on the colonies asked, "If the Americans shall not be permitted to import Iron Duty free, what Course will they, nay must they take, but to manufacture it themselves?"[4] By then the number of colonists had swelled from around fifty thousand in 1650 to around a million and a half. Virginia was the most populous colony, followed in descending order by Massachusetts, Pennsylvania, Maryland, Connecticut, and New

York. Each colony had its own history and distinct character, but the common characteristic of the people in that part of the New World was their individualism and independent spirit.

Troops raised in the colonies serving in the British Army (as opposed to in the colonial militias) were referred to as "Royal Americans." In 1741 in an account of the siege of the Spanish city of Cartagena de Indias in present-day Colombia during the War of Jenkin's Ear (in short, the Spanish cut off Jenkin's ear and a nine-year war followed), *The Scots Magazine* noted that "two battalions of the Americans came on shore . . . but they were obliged to lie three nights upon their arms, for the want of tents and tools, which could not be landed with them."[5]

American militias fighting alongside British regulars in the colonial wars reinforced the American sense of identity. The British officers looked down on the colonials as scruffy ruffians who would not follow orders. The Americans saw the British troops as automatons enslaved to their officers. But free America had a decided appeal to some of the redcoats, and desertion was rampant among the British forces. When a notice about new military legislation in Parliament ran in a London magazine in 1755 under the headline, "Americans Subjected to the Mutiny Act," it was clear to whom the act referred, and why.[6] Earlier that same year when General Braddock was dispatched to the colonies on the eve of the French and Indian War, a farsighted Brit named John Shebbeare observed that the Crown would do well to mind the colonial character. "The Americans are a hard-headed and stubborn race," he wrote, "descended from those fathers, who are great enemies to ministers; they have shewn in the late wars that they dare to fight, and will follow no leaders but those born in their own country: for this reason it may be presumed [the King has] sent them officers from this kingdom, lest being inured to martial affairs under their own countrymen, they may declare themselves independent."[7]

The First American

One of the Americans who supported Braddock's campaign against the French was a Pennsylvania assemblyman named Benjamin Franklin, one of the first citizens of the New World to achieve international fame. Historian H. W. Brand dubbed Franklin "the first American":

> *I use the term in three senses. One is that in his lifetime he was the most illustrious American, he was the best-known American of his day. Secondly, he began a model for the American character. He was practical. He was self-reliant, self-educated, unimpressed with wealth and title, optimistic, he had a sense of humor, and he was a great enthusiast of civic virtue. And thirdly, I see him really as the one to have—the first to have a real sense of an American identity separate from that of Englishmen.*[8]

Franklin was an exceptional product of the new land. He was born in Boston in 1706, the tenth son of a soap maker. He left school in his teens to work at his brother James' pioneering newspaper *The New-England Courant,* where he penned the famous "Silence Dogood" letters. He relocated to Philadelphia when he was seventeen, continuing his writing career, most notably penning *Poor Richard's Almanack,* and earning a reputation as an inventor. He was a model for the Enlightenment-era polymath, engaging in practical inquiries into important scientific questions of the day, famously "discovering" electricity and inventing bifocal lenses and the Franklin stove. He founded Philadelphia's Union Fire Company and pioneered fire insurance. He was involved in public affairs in the colonies and abroad, and testified before Parliament against the Stamp Act. He was a Pennsylvania delegate to the Second Continental Congress and helped write the Declaration of Independence. The words placed in Franklin's mouth by librettist Peter Stone in the 1970 Broadway musical *1776: A Musical Play* ring true both for Franklin's time and our own. When fellow Pennsylvanian John Dickinson asserts that "the people of these colonies maintain a higher regard for their mother country" than a desire for independence, Franklin responds,

> *Higher certainly than she feels for them. Never was such a valuable possession so stupidly and recklessly managed than this entire continent by the British crown. Our industry discouraged, our resources pillaged. Worst of all, our very character stifled. We've spawned a new race here, Mr. Dickinson. Rougher, simpler, more violent, more enterprising, less refined. We're a new nationality. We require a new nation.*[9]

During the Revolution, Franklin played an important role in establishing that new nation. As ambassador to the court of Louis XVI he was instrumental in securing the alliance with France that ultimately led to military victory over the British. He, along with John Adams and John Jay, negotiated and signed the 1783 Treaty of Paris, by which the Crown recognized the United States as "free, sovereign and independent States." Franklin's most important contribution was to help see to it that the Americans were established not only as a people, but also as a country.

The Boundless Frontier

"The American character did not spring full-blown from the Mayflower," Frederick Jackson Turner said. "It came out of the forests and gained new strength each time it touched a frontier." Significantly, he introduced the "Frontier Thesis" at the Columbian Exposition of 1893, honoring the four hundred years since Columbus' voyage. The struggle for survival on the physical frontier established the American identity from its earliest days, and while that struggle has changed, in other respects the frontier is still with us.

The American frontier was a practical source of liberty. Those who ventured into it found a life that was harder, more challenging, less organized, and fundamentally freer. Many who came to the New World were drawn irresistibly from the coasts toward the forests and mountains of the West. The frontier areas were dangerous but the lure of freedom overcame the fear of hazards, both known and unknown.

The colonists' westward drift created political problems for the Crown. After the French and Indian War was settled, London did not want Americans moving west and stirring up yet more trouble. In 1763 a boundary line was draw in an attempt to rein in the wandering Americans, and settlement west of the Appalachian Mountains was prohibited. This was intended to protect the Indians, keep out gunpowder and alcohol, and generally retain Crown control over the land until it could be dealt with in an orderly manner. Under the 1774 Quebec Act, the Northwest Territory, the area between the Ohio River and the Great Lakes, was attached to Quebec, which was given rights to retain French law and Catholicism. But the colonies already claimed much of this land, and parts had been settled. Parliament could not enforce its edicts, and a line on a map in London was meaningless to most Americans.

"The established Authority of any government in America, and the policy of Government at home, are both insufficient to restrain the Americans," noted the royal governor of Virginia, Lord Dunmore. "They acquire no attachment to Place: But wandering about Seems engrafted in their Nature; and it is a weakness incident to it, that they Should for ever imagine the Lands farther off are Still better than those upon which they are already settled." He suggested that there was no easy solution to this problem. "Impressed from their earliest infancy with Sentiments and habits, very different from those acquired by persons of a Similar condition in England, they do not conceive that Government has any right to forbid their taking possession of a Vast tract of Country, either uninhabited, or which Serves only as a Shelter to a few Scattered Tribes of Indians."[10]

After the Revolution, the United States gained title to these territories and the westward expansion continued. The acquisition of the Louisiana Territory also energized the desire of the native-born and immigrants alike to find new opportunities. The expression "Go west, young man," attributed erroneously to Horace Greeley, encapsulated this belief in the frontier as a place of boundless opportunity.

The character developing there was similar to that which had been growing in the earliest days when the frontier was found only miles from the coastline. The Marquis de Talleyrand, who "observed [the American character] closely on the spot," said it was "not fixed." The "woodman and the fisherman" he saw as "the most common specimens of native manners" while "the inhabitants of towns ape the British."[11] Another French traveler, the Duke de La Rochefoucault Liancourt, recounted his experiences meeting Americans of the frontier as follows:

> *We met several families, who had quitted their former habitations in quest of new ones. These transmigrations are generally removals from an old into a new country. The attachment to local property is yet but little known among the Americans. The soil, on which they were born, nay that which they have themselves rendered fit for cultivation, is valued by them little more than any other. Everywhere they live in a simple and frugal manner; their friendly connections also are mostly confined to their own families, which move about with them. Everywhere they can procure whisky and salt pork.*[12]

An English visitor in 1804 noted that "Vermont, Kentucky, and Tennessee are new states, daily receiving the refuse of all the rest.

The inhabitants are almost as unpolished as the Indian natives they have dispossessed."[13] He described Americans thus:

> *Naturally grave, deliberate, and temperate; enterprising, ingenious, and if not scientific, it is owing more to a want of education, than a want of genius. The love of liberty, and impatience of control, break out at a very early period in their youth. Children are too gay, and too delighted with the prospect before them, to be naturally inclined to study; they are for enjoying life, when they should be learning how to enjoy it.*[14]

Explorer Zebulon Pike's journals recorded meeting an Indian "whose countenance expressed great astonishment when told that Mr. Pike was an American; for, it is here confessed that the savages express the greatest veneration for the American character when it is connected with warlike achievements: they say, 'the American is neither a Frenchman nor an Englishman, but a white Indian.'"[15]

Such anecdotes and tales are common in American history throughout the nineteenth century and into the twentieth, in other guises. They capture the restlessness, energy, and strength of the frontiersmen, and the sense of the possible. The frontier represented opportunity and second chances. It was a place to reinvent oneself or find a new life. From the original settlements founded on the Atlantic coast and in eastern virgin forests to the Pacific Ocean missions and outposts that became California, America was always the frontier.

Even with the official closing of the frontier in 1880—which was really just recognition of the fact that the line of settlement had become irrelevant—the idea endured; the spirit was more important than the space. The frontier became—and still is—anywhere people can pursue their dreams. Urbanization and industrialization presented their own new frontiers. Immigrants entered a world that was alien in speech, thought, and manner, and even physically unlike anything they had previously known. They had to struggle to survive and flourish with the same spirit and drive of the pioneers who tamed the wilderness.

The American frontier is also the cutting edge of knowledge, science, technology, and invention. The quote attributed to Director of U.S. Patent Office Charles H. Duell in 1899 that "Everything that can be invented has been invented" is not only untrue, it is patently un-American. The frontier is the unknown, the edge of human imagination. It is something unpredictable and unmanageable. It is expressed in innovation, technological development, economic growth, art, culture, or anything creative. It is the spirit of the pioneer children enjoying life, of the families moving restlessly from farm to farm, of the explorers and inventors. America is still the undiscovered country, the ungoverned space, the limitless opportunity, and its frontier is the future.

Goodbye, Columbus?

The nation and people named for Amerigo Vespucci had not forgotten Christopher Columbus, nor had they forsaken him. Generations honored Columbus who had never heard of Vespucci and never knew the origin of their country's name. His name graces hundreds of places: towns, counties, waterways, schools, parks, and buildings. Columbus was regarded as one of the most heroic and significant figures of his or any age. The "Admiral of the Ocean Seas" was celebrated throughout the Americas as a visionary who braved the unknown on a mission of discovery that created a new world.[16]

Columbus has been honored in the United States for nearly as long as the country has existed. The word "Columbia" (land of Columbus) was coined in 1738, perhaps by Samuel Johnson, and was soon adopted in the colonies. Starting during the Revolution, Columbia was revered as the goddess of freedom, as Lady Liberty. The song "Hail Columbia," the music for which was composed for George Washington's inauguration in 1789, was the unofficial national anthem for over a century, and the seat of government for the new country was named the District of Columbia.

Columbia became synonymous with America, and a few thought the name should be made official. In 1814, Simon Willard Jr. proposed that all of North America join in a new country called the Columbian Union. "It is of the greatest importance that Columbia is the name of our country, and not America," he wrote. "The great name of Columbus, forgotten by Kings, degraded in chains of midnight solitude, while the name of Americus, in his own selfish written books, was open in every tyrant closet, and himself exalted to stations of kingly notice." Willard noted the symbolic importance of the name. "This country in the name of Columbia has no other meaning than the rights of man; it means nothing else from the honest heart of its founder, than union in original right; its constitution proves it; it was never wrote in the name of self, like Americus, but in the name of country for COLUMBUS."[17] Willard believed that the name "Columbia" itself had special redemptive powers. Some felt Columbus should have honorary citizenship; French historian Jean-Jacques Ampère observed that it was "a sorrow for the people of the United States not to be able to claim that an American discovered America."[18]

One of the earliest commemorations of Columbus' historic voyage was in 1792, the three-hundred-year anniversary, organized by the Society of St. Tammany in New York City. Washington Irving's four-volume *A History of the Life and Voyages of Christopher Columbus*, published in 1828, helped popularize the explorer's exploits, and Italian Americans began regular celebrations in various U.S. cities in the mid-nineteenth century. The first national observance was declared in 1892 to commemorate the four hundredth anniversary of Columbus' historic voyage. It fittingly was called Discovery Day, and President Benjamin Harrison asked Americans to "devote themselves to such exercises as may best express honor to the discoverer and their appreciation of the great achievements of the four completed centuries of American life." The Sons of the American Revolution even sought to have Discovery Day declared the "Fourth of July for the world."

The 1893 World's Columbian Exposition in Chicago was a frank celebration of America's technological, cultural, and economic progress. At that time the United States was an emerging power, youthful, muscular, and proud, a growing country facing the world unafraid and unashamed. In 1905, Colorado became the first state to observe an annual Columbus Day holiday. By 1920, the rest of the country had followed, and President Franklin D. Roosevelt set October 12 as the official date of observance in 1937. Columbus Day became a federal holiday only in 1970.

But by then, the reputation of the Genoan mariner was under concerted assault. Columbus fell afoul of the guilt culture of the Sixties. In particular, he was singled out for mockery in the seminal 1969 Native American manifesto, *Custer Died for Your Sins.* Like any other highly regarded figure of history, Columbus was deconstructed with extreme prejudice and redefined as a slaver, a religious bigot, a poor administrator, and a rotten ship's captain. He was not the man of Irving's "hardy genius," "inflexible constancy," and "heroic courage"; he was simply a guy who got lost and lucked out.

Columbus' voyages became a symbol for everything terrible that followed. He was castigated as the first European colonialist. His gift to the New World was not freedom but slavery and disease. He destroyed the idyllic Native American paradise populated by "noble savages" who simply wished to live in peace. Charles Mann, author of *1491*, estimated that over one hundred million Indians died in the first century after Columbus arrived, making "the European conquest of the Americas . . . undoubtedly the most horrific case of genocide in the history of mankind."[19] By the time of the five-hundred-year anniversary of his voyage in 1992, the revisionist view of Columbus was dominant, and the celebration was an anticlimax.

In 2002, Venezuelan dictator Hugo Chavez changed the name of the holiday to "Day of Indigenous Resistance," and two years later activists in Caracas tore down a statue of "Columbus the tyrant." From this perspective, 1492 was nothing to celebrate. It was the beginning of the end.

There is a tinge of hypocrisy in the claims of the Columbus bashers. The year 1491 was no golden age in the soon-to-be New World. Tribes and civilizations fought wars for territory, booty, and slaves. Life was a nightmare for the vanquished, assuming they were even allowed to live. Multiculturalists overlook or explain away the cruel rites of the Aztecs, or the chattel status of women in most pre-Columbian American cultures. The relative lack of advancements in science and technology—even the absence of the wheel—is praised as indicative of the virtue of simplicity, of living in harmony with nature.

Columbus' critics should at least be grateful for the introduction of the horse, which had a decisive impact on the evolution of the culture of the Plains Indians. The horse has become a romantic emblem of Native American life on the Great Plains, but was not widespread in the West until about one hundred years after the founding of the English settlement at Plymouth. In other words, the tradition of the Pilgrims is at least as venerable as anything connected to the mounted Indian, if not more so, judging by date of establishment.

Title to the land had changed hands even before the Europeans arrived. Several successive migratory waves came to the Americas, and one can imagine that when the nomadic bands that arrived nine thousand years ago showed up, those who had wandered in over two thousand years earlier thought, "there goes the neighborhood." Central American empires rose and fell. Settlements along the North American river systems flourished and vanished. Claims of ancient residence sound credible when the only source for their provenance is those who have most recently occupied the land, and there are no written records to prove otherwise. Nevertheless, in some cases we know the bloody chain of custody. The Black Hills, for example, are revered as sacred ground to the Sioux; but three hundred years ago, they were sacred ground to the Kiowa, who lived there on a lease from the previous occupants, the Crow, until the Sioux drove them both out.

Revisionist accounts touting the unblemished virtues of the pre-Columbian era must be approached as skeptically as one-sided accounts of Columbus himself. But even acknowledging the imperfections of the man, Columbus Day is not only, or even principally, a celebration of the mariner but of all that came of his voyages. In the wake of the discovery of the New World, Charles V of Spain adopted as his motto "Plus Ultra," roughly, "More Beyond," in answer to the traditional "Ne Plus Ultra" on the Pillars of Hercules. How much more beyond he could never have fathomed. Columbus unleashed the most significant migration in history, which has led to some of the greatest advancements in politics, trade, technology, the arts, science, and agriculture—the gamut of human endeavor. This was not his intention, of course; what took place in the centuries after his discovery probably would have been beyond his ken. Nevertheless, over the centuries Columbus has become an icon of human imagination, exploration, and discovery, and he has lent his name to the goddess of freedom.

The robust spirit attributed to Columbus, which is fundamental to the American character, is waning. The assault on Columbus is an assault on the idea of America. For many in this country and around the world, the American national identity is defined by guilt, oppression, and a sense of unearned entitlement. A country cannot long survive which doubts itself and condemns its own history. Each generation must renew the sense of discovery that is at the core of what it means to be American. The voyage to a new world continues, but there is no guarantee it will be a better one. Preserving the vision of America as the shining city on a hill requires the boldness of Columbus, the same willingness to take action, to reach into the unknown. These days schools teach that America's national heroes are in fact its villains, presidents curry international favor by apologizing for the country, and climate change fanatics and opponents of free markets say that we must halt our journey or fall off the edge of the earth. But in the words of an old patriotic ballad,

> *Sail on, sail on, Columbia, thy course by wisdom laid,*
> *We trust thy fate, O ship of state, to none who shrink dismayed . . .*
> *May the God of Nations hold thee safe when storms prevail,*
> *And keep the lights which guide thee right, sail on Columbia, sail.*[20]

three

AMERICAN EXCEPTIONALISM

At the G-20 Summit in London in 2009, President Obama was asked about the notion of American exceptionalism and said, "I believe in American exceptionalism, just as I suspect that the Brits believe in British exceptionalism and the Greeks believe in Greek exceptionalism." He went on to clarify: "I think that we have a core set of values that are enshrined in our Constitution, in our body of law, in our democratic practices, in our belief in free speech and equality, that, though imperfect, are exceptional." But the impression was left that Mr. Obama believed that the concept of American exceptionalism was mere nativist prejudice, the sense held by people in every society that they are somehow special.[1]

It is not unusual for people to praise their own country. Every place has its cheerleaders who will argue its virtues, whether justifiable or not. The practice is ancient; the funeral oration delivered by the Athenian leader Pericles honoring the dead in the first year of the Peloponnesian War with Sparta was a glorification of the Athenian *polis* and justification for the continuance of the struggle.[2] (The Spartans characteristically did not need florid orations to know why they were better than the Athenians. To them it was obvious, so why bother saying it?) Kings, emperors, and assorted other potentates throughout history have had their regimes' praises sung, usually on command.

But American exceptionalism does not refer to simple nationalistic boasting, flag-waving, or chanting "U-S-A" at a sporting event. The idea predates the formation of the United States and is a product of a uniquely American culture founded in freedom and pledged to the pursuit of human aspirations. An outsider, former British Prime Minister Margaret Thatcher, stated it well:

> *Americans and Europeans alike sometimes forget how unique is the United States of America. No other nation has been built upon an idea, the idea of liberty. No other nation has so successfully combined people of different races and nations within a single culture. . . . Whether in flight from persecution or from poverty, the huddled masses have, with few exceptions welcomed American values, the American way of life and American opportunities. And America herself has bound them to her with powerful bonds of patriotism and pride.*[3]

The American Zion

The earliest expressions of this exceptional impulse were tied to the idea of Providence; America had a higher purpose. Early settlers, particularly in New England, believed that the land was chosen and prepared by God for his children, and many who arrived believed that it was a Zionist experiment. America was either explicitly part of a divine plan or a tabula rasa on which the God-given or natural potential of man would be revealed. Like Jerusalem, it was to be a "city on a hill, which cannot be hid," a light unto the nations. This current of American thought has long endured. "You can call it mysticism if you want to," Ronald Reagan said, "but I have always believed that there was some divine plan that placed this great continent between two oceans to be sought out by those who were possessed of an abiding love of freedom and a special kind of courage."[4]

John Winthrop, governor of Massachusetts Bay Colony, originated the image of America as the New Jerusalem. In a sermon on the ship *Arabella* in 1630, as the Puritans were readying to make landfall, Winthrop implored the settlers to

> *keep the unity of the spirit in the bond of peace. . . . We shall find that the God of Israel is among us, when ten of us shall be able to resist a thousand of our enemies; when He shall make us a praise and glory that men shall say of succeeding plantations, "may the lord make it like that of New England." For we must consider that we shall be as a city upon a hill. The eyes of all people are upon us.*[5]

Winthrop's views on the workings of Providence would hardly pass contemporary muster. In 1634, after disease had ravaged the Indian tribes surrounding the colony, he wrote a friend in England, "But for the natives in these parts, God hath so pursued them, as for 300 miles space the greatest part of them are swept away by smallpox which still continues among them. So as God hath thereby cleared our title to this place, those who remain in these parts, being in all not 50, have put themselves under our protection."[6]

This view of America as a land ordained by God to be free was called Federal Theology, and reached its highest expression in the works of Ipswich, Massachusetts, preacher John Wise. In 1710 he discussed the nature of just civil government, asserting that "every man must be acknowledged equal to every man," and "the end of all good government is to cultivate humanity and promote the happiness of all and the good of every man in all his rights, his life, liberty, estate, honor, and so forth."[7] His views had significant influence in prerevolutionary America, and even on the phrasing of the Declaration of Independence.

In his first inaugural address, George Washington also echoed the view that Americans were a chosen people:

> *The propitious smiles of Heaven can never be expected on a nation that disregards the eternal rules of order and right which Heaven itself has ordained, and since the preservation of the sacred fire of liberty and the destiny of the Republican model of government are justly considered as deeply, perhaps as finally, staked on the experiment entrusted to the hand of the American people.*[8]

European observers of the American scene noted this sense of being a chosen people. French political thinker Alexis de Tocqueville, after seeing the workings of American democracy in the 1830s, recorded that "for fifty years it has been impressed upon the inhabitants of the United States that they form the only religious, enlightened, and free people. They see that with them, up to the present, democratic institutions prosper, while meeting with failure in the rest of the world; they have then an immense opinion of themselves, and they are not far from believing that they form a species apart from the human race."[9] German philosopher Georg Wilhelm Friedrich Hegel concluded in 1831 that America is "the land of the future, where, in the ages that lie before us, the burden of the World's History shall reveal itself."[10]

The Empire of Liberty

The idea that the mission of the United States is to expand the scope of freedom in the world is as old as the country itself. "I always consider the settlement of America with reverence and wonder,"

John Adams wrote, "as the opening of a grand scene and design in providence, for the illumination of the ignorant and the emancipation of the slavish part of mankind all over the earth."[11] In 1780, Thomas Jefferson wrote to Colonel George Rogers Clark, then commanding Virginia forces in what would become the Northwest Territory, about his vision for post-Revolutionary America. "We shall form to the American union a barrier against the dangerous extension of the British Province of Canada," he wrote, "and add to the Empire of liberty an extensive and fertile Country thereby converting dangerous Enemies into valuable friends."[12] Jefferson envisioned that this "Empire of Liberty" would span the North American continent. Twenty-three years later he partly realized this vision with the Louisiana Purchase, which doubled the size of the young country and extended its western boundary to the Rocky Mountains. And, coincidentally, George Rogers Clark's younger brother William joined with Meriwether Lewis to explore this vast new American domain. Jefferson considered the purchase "a great achievement to the mass of happiness which is to ensue."[13]

In a letter to his successor, James Madison, Jefferson advocated seeking a deal with Napoleon to annex Spanish Cuba to the United States. Then he suggested, "I would immediately erect a column on the Southernmost limit of Cuba & inscribe on it a *Ne plus ultra* as to us in that direction. We should then have only to include the North in our confederacy . . . and we should have such an empire for liberty as she has never surveyed since the creation: & I am persuaded no constitution was ever before so well calculated as ours for extensive empire & self government."[14] Ultimately, Jefferson believed that the nascent Empire of Liberty and American-style freedom would spread to the rest of the globe as a natural expression of progress. "I am eighty-one years of age," he wrote in 1824, "born where I now live, in the first range of mountains in the interior of our country. And I have observed this march of civilization advancing from the seacoast, passing over us like a cloud of light, increasing our knowledge and improving our condition . . . and where this progress will stop no one can say. Barbarism has, in the meantime, been receding before the steady step of amelioration; and will in time, I trust, disappear from the earth."[15] The concept of the Empire of Liberty was a direct extension of the self-evident truths of the Declaration of Independence. If freedom was the birthright of Americans, then it was the right of all people.[16]

A generation later the Empire of Liberty had evolved into the concept of Manifest Destiny. It is credited to John L. O'Sullivan, editor of *United States Magazine and Democratic Review*, and was widely used around the time of the victorious war with Mexico to justify U.S. territorial expansion. The 1848 Treaty of Guadalupe Hidalgo added approximately eight hundred thousand square miles to the United States, an area about as large as the Louisiana Purchase, and included all or part of ten states, notably California and Texas.[17] To proponents of the American mission, the rapid territorial expansion of the United States was truly destiny made manifest. In the wake of the Mexican-American War, poet Henry Wadsworth Longfellow penned his famous ode, "O Ship of State," expressing his belief in the continued unfolding of America's noble future:[18]

Thou, too, sail on, O Ship of State!
Sail on, O Union, strong and great!
Humanity with all its fears,
With all the hopes of future years,
Is hanging breathless on thy fate!

Exporting American Exceptionalism

The James K. Polk administration's settlement of the Oregon boundary issue—which was solved diplomatically, despite the political slogan "Fifty-Four Forty or Fight!"—was the last major acquisition in what would be the lower forty-eight states.[19] In the course of a few generations the United States had grown from the original thirteen states hard against the Atlantic to a nation that spanned from "sea to shining sea." But not everyone was convinced that America required that much space to be exceptional. A Whig opponent of the Polk administration's policies denounced Manifest Destiny as imperialism thus:

> *The progressives, in speeches and newspapers, have for some time been accustomed to speak, with high gratification and delight, of "a good time coming," and not far off, when all Mexico shall be absorbed in our own progressive Republic. They call it our "manifest destiny." . . . They are willing to show the faith they have in the sublimities of Progressive Democracy, by employing the awful agency of war . . . to dismember and despoil Mexico, if they can, of one third of her empire, and annex so much at once to the United States, as a kind of first fruits offered up to the present god of democratic worship—our Manifest Destiny.*[20]

This was an expression of the same tension that today frames the debate about American activism abroad. The question is partly to what extent the American experiment is exportable, but more importantly whether it should be exported. In his farewell address as president, George Washington warned against entangling alliances and advocated remaining aloof from continental power politics. In an oration on July 4, 1821, President John Quincy Adams answered the views of Congressman Henry Clay of Kentucky, who had given a passionate floor speech advocating U.S. recognition of the Greek rebels fighting for freedom from the Turkish Ottoman Empire, the cause célèbre of its day.[21] Adams said that America "goes not abroad in search of monsters to destroy. She is the well-wisher to the freedom and independence of all. She is the champion and vindicator only of her own."[22]

Thus for the first century of its existence, the United States was mostly uninvolved with global politics. It had neither the interests nor the capacity for overseas adventures. In 1832 the Monroe Doctrine sought to insulate the newly free Western Hemisphere from European colonialism. There were notable exceptions, such as the Barbary Wars in North Africa, the opening of Japan, and a variety of smaller incidents taking place in exotic locales.

But with growing power and trade relationships came growing interests, and new capabilities. The bubble of isolationism finally broke in 1898 with the Spanish-American War, which was consciously fought to liberate Cuba, the Philippines, and other vestiges of the old Spanish Empire. The Philippines, in particular, gave the United States its first taste of overseas nation building and its first foreign counterinsurgency.[23] Some years afterward, in the wake of World War I, Woodrow Wilson would seek to "make the world safe for democracy," an idealist experiment that shattered on the realities of global power politics.

Dubbed the "American Century," particularly for U.S. dominance after the Second World War, the twentieth century was driven by both realist and idealist forces. The United States was committed to defending the free world against the menace of international communism, and in practical terms it was the only country that could ensure global stability. The United States in the 1950s was the center of the world. It was an economic powerhouse and enjoyed its largest-ever share of the global economy. It was the driving force in art, culture, invention, and innovation. The country and its ideals were respected throughout the free world, and even more so among the people in the areas that had fallen to communism. Agreements such as the 1948 Universal Declaration of Human Rights seemed to affirm global acceptance of the self-evident truths held in the Declaration of Independence.

But there were clear limits to freedom's frontier. The United States chose to contain communism but not to actively roll it back. The freedom fighters in Budapest in 1956 learned the hard way that the United States was not going to provoke an armed confrontation with the Soviet Union over Hungarian freedom. The lesson was repeated in Czechoslovakia in 1968. The war in Vietnam was finally lost in 1975 because the United States chose to fight it as a limited defensive war rather than to use its overwhelming military superiority to force a peace on Hanoi.[24] In the post-colonial world the United States sometimes found itself backing authoritarian dictators instead of Jeffersonian democracies, with the realist belief that maintaining stability was more important than promoting freedom, and that in any case the regimes would eventually evolve into free states.[25]

The end of the Cold War inspired some to declare the final victory of the Western liberal ideal. In 1989, American political economist Francis Fukuyama proclaimed the "end of history," and it seemed briefly that the future of international relations would be a series of friendly roundtables under the umbrella of a democratic peace.[26] But the old tensions of power politics had not gone away. Not all the dictators of the world bowed to the logic of liberty and went quietly into the night. Suppressed national and ethnic conflicts erupted on the old Soviet periphery. And the rising challenge from Islamist radicalism proved that Western notions of freedom and tolerance were not universally accepted.

Iran and Saudi Arabia never internalized or even considered the Jeffersonian ideal, and began exporting their competing visions of a sharia-based future. The al Qaeda terrorist organization brought the fight against freedom to American soil on September 11, 2001. Free governments were established in Iraq and Afghanistan with the help of American arms, but these conflicts also showed the limits of liberation. And the authoritarian regimes that were swept away by the 2011 Arab Spring are being replaced by Islamist theocracies for which the only self-evident truths are those contained in the Koran. All of this occurred against a backdrop of fading American military power, waning diplomatic influence, and a declining share of the world's economy. Whether or not the United States is the world's single, necessary nation, it is not sufficiently powerful to make humanity free.

The Laboratory of Democracy

The contemporary discussion of American exceptionalism focuses on foreign policy and national security; it is a debate over two visions of the shining city, as either an inspiration for liberty or an active force for liberation. But that is not solely, or even principally, what exceptionalism means. The most important aspect of exceptionalism is the spirit of the people and the drive to continually engage in the American experience.

From its earliest period, America was a place where people could establish self-governing communities and order their affairs in the way they saw fit. Americans lived in enclaves of consensual authoritarianism; communities established their own rules for proper living. Freedom in that sense meant the freedom to organize a community by a particular plan in pursuit of a specific goal. Frequently this was religiously based, such as with the Puritans, the Mormons, or the Anabaptist groups that came to America and formed Amish, Mennonite, and other communities that flourish still. But it could also be based on pursuing economic gain or simply providing a safe and stable home in which families could live and flourish.

There was room enough in the country for all kinds of communities and a general willingness to let each state govern its own affairs. Community standards were important because communities mattered. Those who did not want to live by the local rules were free to try to change them or, failing that, to go elsewhere, to join other communities, to live among the diversity of the cities, or start their own experiments on the frontier. The result was a patchwork of villages, towns, cities, and states, each with its own character based on the beliefs, inclinations, and political views of the people who lived there.

In 1791 the Tenth Amendment to the Constitution recognized this arrangement, and the federal system affirmed the conditional autonomy of the states and the people. America was a hodgepodge of semi-sovereign experiments. Some would succeed and others fail. These "laboratories of democracy" were a national strength, promoting diversity and harmony, and allowing for a variety of forms of social and economic organization for the health and welfare of the citizens.[27] It was a framework for the expression of exceptionalism in countless forms without imposing a particular vision on those who did not accept it. "It is one of the happy incidents of the federal system," wrote Supreme Court Justice Louis Brandeis, "that a single courageous state may, if its citizens choose, serve as a laboratory; and try novel social and economic experiments without risk to the rest of the country."[28] And the democratic system ensured that should an experiment become too odious for the citizenry, they could elect a new government to chart a different course.

In its most developed form the exceptionalist impulse became an active search for human perfectibility. The utopian spirit has always been strong in America. It touched the writings of transcendentalists like Henry David Thoreau, whose *Walden* inspired generations of people seeking to find their own idyllic center. Utopianism also found expression in attempts to build new social organizations. Fruitlands, a transcendentalist commune not far from Walden Pond in Harvard, Massachusetts, lasted a short seven months, broken when the lofty spirit came face to face with poor business planning. Another commune at Brook Farm in West Roxbury lasted a few years. More successful experiments were conducted at Oneida, New York; New Harmony, Indiana; and Icaria, Iowa. Twentieth-century attempts included Arden, Delaware; Freeland, Washington; and numerous nameless attempts to establish communities based on communalism, anarchism, local alternative currencies, organic farming, religious enthusiasm, or free love, among other things. Whether approaching the question from the left, right, or center, with a conscious plan or without, America was the place to be to attempt to perfect humanity—or simply to be left alone.

The downside of the utopian spirit is when it seeks to universalize. Some utopians are not happy unless everyone is living their particular dream. For them, freedom is a means to the end of imposing their standard of virtue. Their authoritarianism is nonconsensual; one either goes along with it or is punished.[29]

Unfortunately, over the last fifty years the coercive utopians have been gaining influence. The gradual breakdown of the federal system, the centralization of political power in Washington, and a gradual extension through litigation of a uniform vision for rights in America has broken down the old concept of freedom. Some see exceptionalism as an ideal that America constantly fails to live up to. They seek to actually perfect the more perfect union, in the manner they have determined is required by all.[30] As commentator Brett Stephens observed, "When a good history of anti-Americanism is someday written, it will note that it's mainly a story of disenchantment—of the obdurate and sometimes vulgar reality of the country falling short of the lover's ideal."[31]

Today, traditional community standards must be balanced against interpretations of the Bill of Rights that differ radically from the intentions of its authors. Supreme Court cases that affirm the value of unique American communities, such as *Wisconsin v. Yoder* (1972), are the exception rather than the rule.[32] Towns that erect traditional religious holiday displays face protests, and the public square featuring a stone carved with the Ten Commandments is a lawsuit waiting to happen. Majority rule has been replaced by the tyranny of the lone malcontent, backed up by a well-funded pressure group and a media campaign. This overweening focus on making the United States into a country where no one could possibly be offended has resulted in the homogenization and coarsening of American public life.

This is the danger of the utopian instinct; it appeals to those who want to impose their view of the perfect society on others and who cannot tolerate diversity of thought or lifestyle. This one-size-fits-all form of collectivism preaches that if America is to be exceptional, it will be so only in their approved manner. It seeks to snuff out the flame of individuality, the inner fire that heats the American soul. The laboratory of democracy requires its citizens to tolerate differences, but, paradoxically, those who most loudly preach tolerance are the most intolerant; those who deify diversity are the quickest to stamp out differences they don't approve of.

One of the best expressions of the American spirit of tolerance came from journalist, soldier, and politician Carl Schurz. He arrived in the United States from Germany in 1852, twenty-three years old and having already lived an eventful life. He was one of the "Forty-Eighters," the revolutionaries on the losing side of the political disruptions that had swept central Europe who found sanctuary in America. He moved to Wisconsin, where he was a lawyer, journalist, and early member of the Republican Party. He served in the Union Army in the Civil War, rising to the rank of Major General of Volunteers and seeing action in some of that conflict's largest battles.

After the war he was elected U.S. Senator from Missouri, and served as Secretary of Interior under President Rutherford B. Hayes. As an immigrant, Schurz saw both the good and bad in America, and was noted for what he called the watchword of true patriotism: "My country, right or wrong; if right, to be kept right; and if wrong, to be set right." But rather than focus on the supposed ability of free people to create the perfect society, he suggested that the land of the free, in reality, is a perfect mirror of the foibles of the flawed humans that make it up:

> *This is humanity when it is free. . . . He who wishes liberty must not be surprised if men do not appear better than they are. Freedom is the only state in which it is possible for men to learn to know themselves, in which they show themselves as*

> *they really are. . . . The will of the people will have its fling and indulge in all kinds of foolishness—but that is its way; if you want to show it the way and then give it liberty of action, it will, nevertheless, commit its own follies. Each one of these follies clears away something, while the wisest thing that is done for the people accomplishes nothing until the popular judgment has progressed far enough to be able to do it for itself.*[33]

American exceptionalism does not spring from a lofty presidential speech seeking to engage the world. It is not found in a forward operating base in Afghanistan, as exceptional as the Americans deployed there are. Exceptionalism exists at home, in the spirit of a free people and in the lives they lead. It is the product of the freedom that makes their lives possible. As journalist Max Lerner said, it is that which is "characteristically American," and "the naked embodiment of the most dynamic elements of modern Western history."[34]

But this is not a given; America is not exceptional by right. John Winthrop, in his 1630 sermon on the deck of the *Arabella*, said that being a light unto the nations was as much a responsibility as a reward, and if the people did not maintain the grace of God, "the Lord will surely break out in wrath against us, and be revenged of such a people, and make us know the price of the breach of such a covenant." The city does not always shine; the hill at times seems a valley. America is not perfect, nor will it ever be. Rather it is in a continual act of becoming. It is this process that makes the country exceptional.

four

THE LAND OF THE FREE

Freedom is a defining aspect of the American character. American liberty was created here, and the struggle to maintain and extend it has been at the heart of American politics ever since. Carl Schurz observed that in America "you can every day see how slightly a people needs to be governed. In fact, the thing that is not named in Europe without a shudder, anarchy, exists here in full bloom. Here are governments, but no rules—governors, but they are clerks. . . . It is only here that you realize how superfluous governments are in many affairs in which, in Europe, they are considered entirely indispensable, and how the possibility of doing something inspires a desire to do it."[1] In no country has freedom been so robust, open-ended, muscular, and disruptive. In 1828 an English writer called the Americans "the most restless, proud, ambitious and quarrelsome people on earth."[2]

Individual self-rule is the fundamental American characteristic. It pervades politics, economics, the arts, and personal behavior. It is the idea that nothing can or should be done without one's consent. The American is a sovereign being, admitting no born superiors—a belief that broke from centuries of tradition handed down from feudal Europe. As Jefferson wrote in 1826, a few weeks before his death, "the mass of mankind has not been born with saddles on their backs, nor a favored few booted and spurred, ready to ride legitimately, by the grace of God."[3] In a 2008 poll that asked what it means to be an American, freedom was mentioned 59 percent of the time, followed by the closely related patriotism (23%) and democracy (16%).[4]

Ayn Rand, the influential twentieth-century author who fled Bolshevik Russia in 1925 and emigrated to America, wrote that the focus on the individual in the founding of the United States made it "the first moral society in history."

> *All previous systems had regarded man as a sacrificial means to the ends of others, and society as an end in itself. The United States regarded man as an end in himself, and society as a means to the peaceful, orderly, voluntary co-existence of individuals. All previous systems had held that man's life belongs to society, that society can dispose of him in any way it pleases, and that any freedom he enjoys is his only by favor, by the permission of society, which may be revoked at any time. The United States held that man's life is his by right (which means: by moral principle and by his nature), that a right is the property of an individual, that society as such has no rights, and that the only moral purpose of a government is the protection of individual rights.*[5]

The Birth of Freedom

America's natural and radical individualism gave rise to a distinct type of character and politics. When Jefferson wrote, "We hold these truths to be self-evident," he was saying that what followed was beyond argument, a premise that one could either accept or reject, but which was fully accepted in America. Whether one thought that freedom derived from God or nature, it was agreed that it was something inborn and inalienable.

American notions of freedom have many roots. Roman political theory rejected the Greek notion that humans were naturally part of communities, the instinctive "political animals" that Aristotle wrote about. The Romans believed humans were creatures who were aware of their self-interest and that free people had the ability to give consent to living under law as part of a community of interests. The bond of law, the *vinculum juris,* is what united the people. The feudal system, which succeeded Roman law in Europe, lost the focus on the individual but retained the notion of the contract as the basis for order and political legitimacy. Feudal government was a complex series of reciprocal relationships in which even the king did not theoretically wield absolute and arbitrary power. The Magna Carta, which English King John was forced to agree to by his rebellious barons in 1215, affirmed that free men held rights under law and the sovereign will was limited by the liberties of his subjects. Though in practice the original document was soon superseded and reissued in various, more limited forms, it became a potent symbol for later generations who sought to limit the powers of the absolutist monarchs.

One of the earliest mentions of America in European political writing refers to it as a haven for those seeking freedom. In a 1535 commentary on the book of Deuteronomy, in particular, on the need to impose the death penalty on blasphemers, Protestant theologian John Calvin wrote:

> *Some insist that since the offense consists only in words, there is no need for such severity. But we muzzle dogs, and shall we leave men free to open their mouths as they please? Those who object are like dogs and swine. They murmur they will go to America where nobody will bother them.*[6]

Ironically, Calvinism, through Presbyterianism and its branches, was so influential in the founding of the American colonies that nineteenth-century German historian Leopold von Ranke concluded, "John Calvin was the virtual founder of America." The New England version of social contract theory can be traced to Calvin. It went through Scotland where John Knox amended it, then emerged on the shores of the New World modeled on the agreement God made with the Israelites. This sense of freedom, and particularly the freedom not to be bothered (much less executed for blasphemy), is central to the concept of America.[7]

From Federal theology came the idea that society exists as a contract. It was not primarily an American notion—the Roundheads during the English Civil War (1642–1651) had agitators preaching this theory in every military unit to justify the right to participate in a revolution against the Crown. But the discovery of the New World had a major impact on the imaginations of European political thinkers. The social contract theorists saw in America the ungoverned "state of nature" that formed the starting point for their theoretical construct. "In the beginning the whole world was America," wrote John Locke in 1689. By that he meant an untouched wilderness free of government. Forty years earlier Thomas Hobbes, in a famous passage in *Leviathan*, had described "mere nature" as a state of "continual fear, and danger of violent death; and the life of man, solitary, poor, nasty, brutish, and short." And while Hobbes believed that such a condition never existed generally all over the world, "the savage people in many places of America, except the government of small families, the concord whereof dependeth on natural lust, have no government at all, and live at this day in that brutish manner."[8]

Hobbes was wrong about the lack of government among the Indians, who had varying degrees of social organization. Indeed the notion of the "noble savage" who lived in splendid natural anarchy became something of a holy grail for anthropologists, and was sought around the world for centuries, but never found.

Yet even before Hobbes the notion of a state of nature where men were or became free simply by being there was alive in the minds of the common people.

In June 1609 the Royal Virginia Company's flagship the *Sea Venture* was leading a fleet of seven ships on a supply mission to the new colony at Jamestown. A storm blew up and the ships were separated. After several days the *Sea Venture* was grounded on the reefs of Bermuda to save it from foundering. Passengers and crew numbering 150 people and a dog made landfall on the Isle of the Devils and were forced to survive as best they could.[9] But after six months ashore, some of the crew, among them a clerk named Stephen Hopkins, mutinied against the leadership of the company. They reasoned that because they were not in the chartered domain of the Virginia Company, they were in a state of nature, thus should be free to choose their own leaders and do as they please. The mutiny failed and Hopkins was sentenced to death. He begged for his life and was spared. Later the survivors fashioned ships to continue their voyage, and Hopkins spent several years in Jamestown before returning to England.[10]

Fast-forward to 1620 and the good ship *Mayflower* carrying the Pilgrims, also under the charter of the Virginia Company, which had authority north to the mouth of the Hudson River. But the ship was blown off course and wound up off the coast of Cape Cod. There followed some "discontented and mutinous speeches that some of the strangers amongst them had let fall from them in the ship: that when they came ashore they would use their own liberty, for none had power to command them."[11] Coincidentally, among the passengers was the former castaway Stephen Hopkins.

William Bradford immediately wrote up a document in which the signatories agreed, "solemnly and mutually, in the presence of God, and one of another, [to] covenant and combine our selves together into a civil body politic, for our better ordering and preservation and furtherance of the ends aforesaid; and by virtue hereof to enact, constitute, and frame such just and equal laws, ordinances, acts, constitutions and offices, from time to time, as shall be thought most meet and convenient for the general good of the Colony, unto which we promise all due submission and obedience." The Mayflower Compact was thus an original, genuine, literal, and specific social contract that predated the writings of Hobbes and Locke by decades. As for Stephen Hopkins, he lived well in the New World, although he later ran afoul of the authorities by opening one of the New World's first taverns. It was another of his significant contributions in the development of American liberty.

Liberty By Neglect

"The society that developed on this side of the Atlantic in the 17th and 18th centuries was a unique phenomenon in world history," scholar and presidential advisor John P. Roche wrote. While the British were engaged in internal revolution and external war, the colonists in the New World "were engaged in a do-it-yourself enterprise in nation-building."[12] In the Old World, people presented problems to the traditional political elites for resolution. But those elites were too far away to play a day-to-day role in the colonies, so people in the colonies began to resolve their issues on their own. In the process they discovered they didn't need the Old World elites. This became America's formula for freedom.

The nascent spirit of liberty in the American colonies was nourished by decades of neglect from the home country. The sheer distance of the colonies from England made managing affairs there problematic, even in the best of times. "Three thousand miles of ocean lie between you and them," Edmund Burke said in Parliament in 1775, seeking conciliation with the colonies. "No contrivance can prevent the effect of this distance in weakening government. Seas roll and months pass between the order and the execution; and the want of a speedy explanation of a single point is enough to defeat the whole system."[13] In addition, the period from 1609 to around 1755 was hardly ideal for managing these faraway lands. England went through a civil war and the overthrow of the monarchy, the Cromwell interregnum, the restoration of the monarchy, and another revolution. There were three Anglo-Dutch wars, six Anglo-French wars, an outbreak of plague, and the Great Fire of London. Against this backdrop, America was largely an afterthought.

There was little reason to be concerned with the Americans anyway. The colonies were not like the Spanish possessions in Central and South America, which seemed to supply limitless gold and silver booty. At first, the British possessions in America struggled to be economically viable. Tobacco came to the rescue of Virginia, though even before the founding of the town that bore his name, King James I, in his pamphlet "A Counterblaste to Tobacco," described smoking as "a custom loathsome to the eye, hateful to the nose, harmful to the brain, dangerous to the lungs, and the black stinking fume thereof, nearest resembling the horrible Stygian smoke of the pit that is bottomless." Other colonies struggled to maintain even subsistence economies in their earliest years.

Politically, the colonies were very different from England. In 1643 Parliament granted dissident theologian Roger Williams a patent for the Rhode Island Province of Plantations, which allowed for self-rule by majority consent. As John P. Roche observed, that was the kind of idea that could get one hanged if discussed too loudly in England. The 1647 Massachusetts Body of Liberties laid out the notion of consent to the rule of law in a way similar to what Locke would do forty years later to justify the 1689 Glorious Revolution. By 1680 in New England there was mass male political participation with few limitations.

A century before the American Revolution, the colonies were already among the freest places on earth. Most people lived better than they had or could possibly have lived in Europe. There were fewer economic controls—no functioning internal mercantilism, guilds, ancient charters, or fixed economy—which meant a field day for artisans and traders to create, innovate, buy, sell, make profits, and ask for or offer higher wages. Outside of the slavery-based plantations there were relatively few rich people and few poor people. Even the indentured servants were self-starters, willing to sign on for seven years of hard labor just to gain passage to the New World and eventual freedom.

Coming to America required an intense personal drive. The people at the roots of the national identity were self-selected freedom seekers, and the result was a society that emphasized the individual. Those who came to America had courage. They were adventurers, seekers, nonconformists, and dreamers. They were the type of people Steve Jobs referred to as "the crazy ones, the misfits, the rebels, the troublemakers, the round pegs in the square holes . . . the ones who see things differently and are crazy enough to think they can change the world."[14] But the earliest Americans were not out to change the world. They were self-generated, self-selected, a people who came here for a purpose. They were out to save themselves, or their souls. Changing the world came later.

The fact that the colonists were surviving—even flourishing—at the ragged edge of civilization built a sense of community that was not commonly found in established Europe. The colonists had a dynamism and vitality derived from the knowledge that they were prospering because of their own efforts. And with this came the sense that they had earned the right to freedom and self-government. The generations born in the New World, who had never known the social, political, and economic limitations imposed on people in the mother country, were particularly imbued with the sense of freedom as a birthright.

Occasionally London took notice. In 1661 a royal agent in Massachusetts named Samuel Maverick complained that the Americans lacked a sense of loyalty. Charles II dispatched a commission in 1664 to investigate. Rather than cooperate with the commissioners, the Puritan government in Massachusetts denied their authority. After a fruitless stay in America they left, and nothing further happened. In 1686 King James II supplanted the Massachusetts government under the Body of Liberties and replaced it with the more centralized Dominion of New England. Crown agent Edward Randolph discovered that Americans paid no attention to British navigation laws and generally did not feel bound by any such rules unless they benefited them. Randolph attempted to enforce the laws and collect duties, but the locals resisted him. The 1689 Glorious Revolution ended his efforts; King James was overthrown, the Body of Liberties was restored, and Randolph was sent back to England in chains.[15]

Americans had come to feel that the Crown had no business meddling in their affairs. If there were problems in the colonies, the locals would resolve them. And for the most part the Crown did not do much meddling. Events on the European continent were much more important. The so-called Second Hundred Years' War with France had broken out. Troops that would have been needed to pacify America were not available. And the Crown did not lose much revenue by not enforcing the navigation laws and other regulations. The colonies were remote and relatively unimportant. Getting anything done there took a long time and was not worth the effort. During the Whig Supremacy in Parliament in the mid-eighteenth century, the government pursued a policy of salutary neglect—so long as the colonies were not causing trouble they could go their own way. However, this policy was simply recognition of matters as they were; as John Adams said, the king had no more real control of affairs in America than he did over the plains of Tartary.

The American Revolution

The American Revolution was not the birth of freedom in this country, but the defense of freedoms that had already been established. Some thought the idea of the colonies going their own way was preposterous. "A Confederacy of such different discordant Settlements gave you an Idea of a monstrous Piece of Patchwork," the *London Public Advertiser* proclaimed in 1775, "ill tacked together with a hot Needle and burnt Thread."[16] But some overseas observers understood that the motivating spirit of freedom in the colonies was the same that had secured British liberty. After a vote in both houses of Parliament formally to declare the colonies in rebellion, the *London Evening Post* called the proclamation "the silliest paper that ever was wrote." It called on the Parliament to "avow that the American struggle is on the same principles that enforced the [Glorious] Revolution; and the public esteem and venerate those noble patriots, and embrace their sentiments."[17] Edmund Burke said in Parliament, "We can not, I fear, falsify the pedigree of this fierce people, and persuade them that they are not sprung from a nation in whose veins the blood of freedom circulates. . . . An Englishman is the unfittest person on earth to argue another Englishman into slavery."[18]

The chain of events that led to the first shots fired on the Lexington green began twenty years earlier. In April 1755 the Congress of Alexandria convened at the home of John Carlyle in Alexandria, Virginia. It was the first intercolonial meeting, called to discuss the brewing conflict with France, later known in America as the French and Indian War (1754–1763). The governors of Virginia, Maryland, Pennsylvania, New York, and Massachusetts met with Major General Edward Braddock, commander-in-chief of the British army in North America. Also present were young militia leader Richard Henry Lee (who would submit the resolution for independence at the Continental Congress in June 1776), Benjamin Franklin (who seemed to turn up everywhere), and twenty-three-year-old Colonel George Washington of the Virginia militia.

The previous year, Virginia governor Robert Dinwiddie, whose colony claimed vast areas of Ohio that were in fact controlled by France, had sent militia units under the leadership of Colonel Washington to confront French troops. They were defeated at the Battle of Fort Necessity and withdrew to Virginia on July 4. Dinwiddie supported intervention by British regulars to clear out the French and open the way for settlement. But the colonies were unwilling to pay for the venture. The governors rebuffed a demand from the British Parliament that they front the money for the war. At Carlyle House, Braddock inadvertently conceived the idea that would become the primary catalyst of the revolution. In a letter to British state secretary Thomas Robinson, Braddock wrote, "I cannot but take the liberty to represent to you the necessity of laying a tax upon all his Majesty's dominions in America, agreeably to the result of Council, for reimbursing the great sums that must be advanced for the service and interest of the colonies in this important crisis."[19]

Four months later Braddock was killed at the Battle of the Monongahela, which opened the war with France and made Washington, who took command after Braddock was killed, a national hero. Thus from the 1755 meeting at Carlyle House in Alexandria came the cause of the revolution, the idea of a colonial congress, and the meeting of three of the central players in the founding of the United States: Washington, Franklin, and Lee.

After the war with France ended in 1763, Braddock's proposed taxes arrived. The British Parliament, then not in Whig hands, constructed a thorough taxation system designed to impose complete control over the colonies. All manner of things were to be taxed—sugar, legal documents, petitions, newspapers, dice, and wine, among other things. The taxes had to be paid in sterling, not local currency. But there was a shortage of British coin, so even if people wanted to pay the tax they would not have been able to in most cases. Had it been fully implemented, this system would have ground much colonial economic activity to a halt.

The tax had a unifying effect on the colonists because it threatened the mainstays of the political class, particularly lawyers, merchants, and newspapermen. The Stamp Act Congress of 1765 attracted fifty delegates from nine colonies. By then, John Roche observed, "we had clearly the most participatory society in the world. The colonies were used to the authority of their own elected assemblies, judges were local men, the population was armed, and direct democracy was guaranteed by the jury system. In short, the provinces were run by local elites who took their authority for granted."[20]

The British printed the stamps and sought tax collectors among the Americans. In general the colonists had three choices—obey the act, refuse to do business under its terms, or ignore it and carry on as usual. They chose the third. No stamp master in the colonies would enforce the act, either out of patriotism or fear, and ultimately the stamps were not purchased or used, or even landed from the ships bringing them from England. When the Whigs came back into power in 1765, Parliament repealed the act, though with the proviso that they maintained the right to pass other such acts in the future.

The future was not long in coming. The Tories came back into power eighteen months later and began to reimpose controls. To sidestep the taxation issue (in part because of the "no taxation without representation" debate, but more to the point because it didn't work) Parliament instead imposed trade duties. Some, such as John Dickinson in his "Letters from a Pennsylvania Farmer," objected that this was really a tax by another name, to no avail. So the colonists resorted to a boycott. Americans stopped buying British goods, which hurt British businesses and created a strong pro-American business lobby in London.

But all of the measures pursued by the government to impose control on the unruly colonies were to no effect. The matter had already been settled. "The Revolution was effected before the war commenced," John Adams said, "in the hearts and minds of the people." The decades of managing their own affairs and the generations that had grown up habituated to liberty had brought forth a new nation and a new people. America was already a fact. "This radical change in the principles, opinions, sentiments, and affections of the people," Adams wrote, "was the real American Revolution."[21] And the right of people to run their own affairs is something they will fight for. Edmund Burke, arguing in Parliament for conciliation with the colonies, was one of the first to affirm the emergence of the American spirit. "This fierce spirit of liberty is stronger in the English Colonies, probably, than in any other people of the earth," he said. "The question is not whether their spirit deserves praise or blame. What, in the name of God, shall we do with it?"[22]

By 1770 pressure from the business lobby in London convinced Parliament to remove all the duties imposed on the Americans, except one that was retained for symbolic reasons and in order to maintain London's right to lay duties: the tax on tea.

five

TEA PARTIES AND PATRIOTISM, OLD AND NEW

On February 18, 2009, at a speech in Mesa, Arizona, President Obama announced the creation of the $75 billion Homeowner Affordability and Stability Plan. The program was intended to address the ongoing housing crisis. "The American dream is being tested," he said, "by a home mortgage crisis that threatens not only the stability of our economy but also the stability of families and neighborhoods. It is a crisis that strikes at the heart of the middle class: The homes in which we invest our savings, build our lives, raise our families, and plant roots in our communities."[1]

The next day on financial network CNBC's "Squawk on the Street," commentator Rick Santelli vigorously denounced the plan from the floor of the Chicago Mercantile Exchange, saying it was a bailout to "subsidize the losers." He criticized it as another wasteful program responding to a crisis created by government interference in the marketplace.[2] "We're thinking of having a Chicago Tea Party!" Santelli shouted, to the applause of traders. "All you capitalists that want to show up at Lake Michigan, I'm gonna start organizing. . . . We're going to be dumping in some derivative securities!"

In that moment a new patriotic movement was born. The inchoate discontent of citizens alarmed by the speed and scope of the Obama administration's intervention in the American economy found a theme, and a mission. The grass roots responded. A week later there were Tea Party–themed protests in forty-eight cities. Santelli later said he was "taken aback to the *N*th power," by the response to his off-the-cuff remarks. "I'd said many things like that on previous episodes," he said, but he "didn't have an inkling" that he would give birth to a political movement because he "said the words *Tea Party*."[3]

The Boston Tea Party

The Tea Party movement used the symbols and myths of the Boston Tea Party as an evocative and convenient framework for mobilizing discontent. It did not arise literally to emulate the events of the eighteenth century. Critics such as E. J. Dionne focused on supposed disconnects between the contemporary movement and the original event. "Whether they intend it or not," he wrote, "their name suggests they believe that the current elected government in Washington is as illegitimate as was a distant, unelected monarchy."[4] He claimed the Tea Partiers had taken the wrong lessons from history, but Dionne confused imagery with substance, as though the movement was really all about wearing tricorn hats and carrying muskets. Other critics simply needed a history lesson. At an October 2010 Tea Party Express event in Reno, Nevada, Sarah Palin urged attendees to "party like it's 1773." This prompted PBS commentator Gwen Ifill and leftist blogger Markos Moulitsas to launch tweets mocking the former GOP vice presidential nominee for her supposed "gaffe" in getting the date wrong. "She's so smart," Mr. Moulitsas wrote sarcastically. But she was smarter than him, since the Boston Tea Party took place on December 16, 1773.[5]

The Boston Tea Party is a legitimate symbol of American resistance to government meddling. It was sparked by the 1773 Tea Act, which Parliament had passed to help alleviate the financial woes of the British East India Company. Complexities of the mercantile system, along with taxes imposed by the 1767 Townshend Acts, had made East India Company tea too expensive to compete with smuggled Dutch tea in the colonies. The Tea Act, aspects of which were proposed by Benjamin Franklin, actually lowered the price of tea. But the Townshend duties were left in place, and by accepting the tea the colonists would also be accepting Parliament's tax, thus implicitly agreeing to taxation without representation. To the American political elite, not to mention the tea smugglers, acquiescence was unacceptable. Besides, as John P. Roche observed, the slogan "No taxation without representation" really meant "No taxation."

Protest meetings against the Tea Act were held at all major American ports. In Philadelphia, a resolution was passed that "whoever shall, directly or indirectly, countenance this attempt, or in any wise aid or abet in unloading, receiving, or vending the tea sent, or to be sent out by the East-India Company while it remains subject to the payment of a duty here, is an enemy to America."[6] In Boston three tea ships docked—the *Dartmouth*, the *Eleanor*, and the *Beaver*—but thousands of protestors prevented them from unloading any tea. However, Massachusetts Royal Governor Thomas Hutchinson would not allow the ships to leave port without paying a duty. A standoff resulted, and a deadline was forcing action. Under the law, the government could confiscate a ship's cargo if it remained twenty days or more in port without paying the duty. The *Dartmouth*'s final day to make payment was December 16. A final mass meeting was held imploring the governor to let the ship depart, to no effect. That night, according to an account in the British press,

> *A number of resolute men (dressed like Mohawks or Indians) determined to do all in their power to save their country from the ruin which their enemies had plotted, in less than four hours emptied every chest of tea on board the three ships . . . amounting to 342 chests, into the sea without the least damage done to the ships or any other property. The masters and owners are well pleased that their ships are thus cleared, and the people are almost universally congratulating each other on this happy event.*[7]

London met this act of revolutionary vandalism with quick retribution. Parliament passed a series of Coercive (or Intolerable) Acts closing the port of Boston until the tea was paid for, and imposing other punishments. Benjamin Franklin pragmatically suggested the debt be paid, but the crisis had begun to escalate, and the two sides became entrenched. Anger over the Intolerable Acts led the First Continental Congress to convene on September 5, 1774, and the following April 19 the Massachusetts minutemen made their stands at Lexington and Concord against British regulars intent on seizing the militia's munitions. Although the Boston Tea Party did not cause the American Revolution, it was one of the catalytic events that made open conflict inevitable.

Subsequent events overshadowed the Boston Tea Party, but it remained a source of local pride in New England. At a Fourth of July gathering in 1805 at Harmony Grove in Lyme, Connecticut, a toast was offered to the Tea Party: "Thirty-one years since, our fathers' patriotism deprived our mothers of the use of tea—may our mothers' tea never deprive us of our fathers' patriotism."[8]

Nostalgia for the Boston Tea Party began to grow after the 1820s as the generation that fought the Revolution began to fade, most notably John Adams and Thomas Jefferson, who both died on July 4, 1826. Obituaries of Tea Partiers and notes like the following from *The New England Farmer* began to pop up in publications across the country:

> *One of the party of "about forty unknown people, dressed like Indians," who boarded the ship Eleanor, in Boston, in 1773, and threw overboard 114 chests of tea, now lives in Cincinnati, Ohio. He is, says the Crisis, a temperate, hardy old veteran, supports his family by the sweat of his brow, and often boasts of the "Boston Tea Party."*[9]

Writer James Hawkes greatly popularized the tale in 1834.[10] He wrote a book based on an interview with ninety-nine-year-old George Hewes of Ostego, New York, who claimed to be one of the last surviving Tea Partiers and also present at the Boston Massacre in 1770. Hawkes painted the impact of the Tea Party in grandiose terms:

> *America seemed destined to be the only spot where the principles of universal reformation could commence their progress; it was there the first blow was to be struck, which, to tyrants through the world, should echo as the knell of their departing hour. The single event of destroying a few thousand pounds of tea, by throwing it into the water, was of itself of inconsiderable importance in American history; but in its consequences, it was, doubtless, one in the series of events, destined to change, and probably improve the condition, not only of our posterity, but of mankind in all ages to come.*[11]

The Boston Tea Party was solidified as part of the American mythos, waxing in popularity through the nineteenth century, then waning after 1900, with a surge in the 1930s and another around the bicentennial. It was periodically evoked in protests, but references to the Boston Tea Party had dropped to a quarter of their peak use by the start of the twenty-first century.[12]

The Return of the Tea Party

Rick Santelli's rant in February 2009 fired the imagination of millions who were uneasy about the direction the country was taking. The fast-moving events of the previous six months—financial collapse, a presidential election, and immediate steps by the incoming administration to make good on its promise to "fundamentally transform" America—had conjured alarm and uncertainty among many Americans, particularly on the conservative side of the spectrum. The symbol of the Boston Tea Party reached back to the earliest days of the founders, when the revolution against Parliamentary excesses was still brewing. It was one of the first cases of direct action taken against the authority of the Crown. The Boston Tea Party was the spark that lit the flame; it was the moment when the colonists took a stand. They acted. They said "no more."

Over the next twenty months, scores of loosely affiliated Tea Party and patriotic groups organized across the country. Hundreds of thousands of people flocked to rallies, engaged in online activism, wrote letters to Congress, and participated in the political process. The Tea Party groups were not centrally organized, directed or funded, but were motivated and united by a common defense of American core beliefs in limited government, economic liberty, and the preservation of the American dream.

The Tea Party movement came under immediate fire from defenders of the Obama administration's agenda, who charged them with everything from extremism to violence to racism. Former House Speaker Nancy Pelosi likened the demonstrators to Nazis, and *Washington Post* columnist Eugene Robinson saw "no coincidence" in "the birth of a big, passionate national movement—overwhelmingly white and lavishly funded—that tries its best to delegitimize . . . the first African-American president."[13] The charge of racism was persistent but unfounded; the low point was in March 2010 when Representative Andre Carson, Indiana Democrat, called an impromptu press conference to charge that protesters of "Obamacare" (the federal Patient Protection and Affordable Care Act) shouted racial slurs at black members of Congress walking from the Cannon House Office Building to the Capitol. Many reporters rushed these charges out uncritically and without investigation, but a video of the event showing the representatives in their staged walk revealed no such epithets being used. In another incident, Representative Emanuel Cleaver II, Missouri Democrat, claimed a protester spat on him, and that the assailant was arrested by Capitol Police. Mr. Cleaver said he declined to file charges, but police spokesperson Sergeant Kimberly Schneider said no arrests were made that day, and no eyewitnesses came forward to substantiate the story.[14] Commentator Andrew Breitbart offered $100,000 to anyone who would come forward with proof of the allegations, but the money went unclaimed.

These unfounded charges played off of the social stereotype of the Tea Party favored by Democratic politicians and liberal commentators: that they were white, redneck, less educated, lower-middle class rabble rousers. But an April 2010 Gallup survey showed that with respect to "their age, educational background, employment status, and race—Tea Partiers are quite representative of the public at large."[15] A *New York Times* poll revealed that members of the movement were "wealthier and more well-educated than the general public." The poll noted that the Tea Partiers' views "are like the general public's in many ways" but their "fierce animosity toward Washington, and the president in particular, is rooted in deep pessimism about the direction of the country." Their three main concerns were "the recent health care overhaul, government spending and a feeling that their opinions are not represented in Washington."[16]

A *USA Today* survey showed that the defining attitudes of Tea Party supporters also closely tracked to the core American ideals. Ninety-two percent believed that "the federal government debt is a very serious/extremely serious threat to the nation's future well-being," 85 percent believed "the size and power of the federal government are a very/extremely serious threat to the nation's future well-being," and 90 percent were "dissatisfied with the way things are going in this country."[17]

The Tea Party was a successful grassroots movement that helped blunt the momentum of the big government programs being pursued by President Obama and Congressional Democrats. The 2010-midterm elections turned into a repudiation of the "hope and change" agenda of 2008. The House elections were a historic defeat for the Democrats. They lost 63 seats, the worst midterm drubbing since 1938, and with them their majority. On the Senate side the Republicans gained six seats, the best showing of any party since 1994. But the Tea Party played a spoiler role in some races, knocking out establishment candidates in primary challenges or dividing conservative voters, resulting in some unexpected wins for the Democrats. However the spirit and vitality of the movement motivated millions of Americans to get involved in politics and push back against a relentlessly growing government.

American Patriots

"Patriotism" has become a fighting word in America. Conservatives use it as an emblem of devotion to America and to the principles on which the country is founded. Liberals counter that true patriots are those who seek change and promote social justice. For every Tea Party patriot there is a member of the left-wing Occupy movement claiming the same mantle. The debate over patriotism is expressed in terms that show deep division, animosity, and anger. It is far from the avowedly patriotic vision of politics George Washington spoke of in his first inaugural address:

> *I trust that no separate view, nor party animosities, will misdirect the comprehensive and equal eye which ought to watch over the great assemblage of communities and interests: so, on another, that the foundations of our national policy will be laid in the pure and immutable principles of private morality; and the preeminence of free government, be exemplified by all the attributes which can win the affections of its citizens, and command the respect of the world. I dwell on this prospect with every satisfaction which an ardent love for my country can inspire.*[18]

While many people associate the word "patriot" with the American revolutionaries, it has a much older vintage. "Patriot" is derived from the Latin *patria*, or fatherland, and in the narrowest sense can refer to simple loyalty to one's place of birth. In politics it means being devoted to the common good above particular interests. This was summed up in a broadside published before Parliament was about to convene in 1731 entitled *"THE British PATRIOT, Or a Timely CAVEAT Against giving into the MEASURES Of any Evil and Corrupt Minister."*[19]

The Roman senator Marcus Tullius Cicero was revered as the archetype of patriotism, a man who gave his life tying to preserve the Roman Republic at the onset of the rule of the Caesars. He was noted not only for his intellect and oratorical skills but also for his devotion to liberty and the common weal. Like many of the Founding Fathers, he was both a critical thinker and a practical politician. John Adams said of Cicero that "All the ages of the world have not produced a greater statesman and philosopher united in the same character."[20] In an eighteenth-century translation of his works, Cicero remarks,

> *The Patriot has always a good Cause, the Cause of his Country and of Mankind, of all others the most important and interesting. His Aim is virtuous, his Ends noble, and therefore all his Pursuits pleasing. The Integrity and laudable Thoughts of his Heart, are a continual Cordial and Support. A Passion for the Public, and the Welfare of Mankind, animates him; the Sense of his Duty fortifies him. He has the Wishes, the Concurrence and Praises of all worthy Men: Opposition from the Vicious and Unworthy, proves a Justification to him, and inspires him with fresh Vigour. His Views are great, benevolent, elevated, even to promote and defend whatever is lovely, righteous, desirable, and praise-worthy in the World; for, the Root of all this is Liberty.*[21]

In early eighteenth-century Britain, the term "patriot" was debated as hotly and loudly as it is today. In June 1734 a magazine printed a laudatory ode to Robert Walpole, who is generally acknowledged as the politician who established the office of prime minister. "The True Patriot," it proclaimed, "He that is wise, just, temperate and brave, Has all the virtues that a man need have. . . . Happy are we since they on Walpole wait, Walpole who guides the helm, and steers the ship of state."[22] But Walpole's opponents painted him as an excessively partisan Whig, dubbing his insular ruling faction the "Court Party," opposed to the "Country Party" of Tories and disaffected liberals. They styled themselves as the true patriots, and claimed to support the good of the country as a whole rather than the narrow factional interests championed by Walpole and his cronies.

Partisan bickering between elected officials gave the monarchists an opening to seize the mantle of patriotism for themselves. They argued that regardless of what was going on in the divisive world of partisan politics, the sovereign rose above it. In January 1734 the *London Evening Post* reported an "Ode for the New Year" performed for King George II, which began:

To GEORGE, to GEORGE, our Patriot King,
The new and happy Season sing!

Colley Cibber, poet laureate to the king, wrote the song the previous year. The *Grub-Street Journal* commented that Cibber was "the first author I have met with, who joins the terms 'patriot' and 'king' together." The *Journal* was uncertain, given "the seeming inconsistency of the terms," whether the Cibber meant "patriot king" as a satirical comment, but acknowledged that it might be proper when "an invidious distinction of Court and Country party is propagated throughout the nation, representing the leaders of the latter as the only true patriots, and those of the former as a set of corrupt men, carrying on an interest very different from that of their own country." [23]

The bitter factionalism in British politics strengthened the notion that the monarch was best suited to bring continuity to government. Henry St. John, Viscount Bolingbroke, a Tory politician and philosopher whose thinking was very influential with the American revolutionaries, argued (following Aristotle) that the rule of a limited, publicly interested, and virtuous "patriot king" was the best form of government. He said that such a monarch was "the most uncommon of all phenomena in the physical or moral world," but "nothing can so surely and so effectually restore the virtue and public spirit essential to the preservation of liberty and national prosperity, as the reign of such a prince."[24]

Ironically King George III, the scourge of the American revolutionaries, was hailed as a patriot before they were. In January 1761, a few months after he ascended the throne, a new ode declared,

Behold a youth now mounts the British throne,
Whom every royal virtue calls her own!
Proceed, great Prince, a Patriot King complete,
And George the Third henceforth be George the Great.[25]

The term "American patriots" was used as early as 1770, but was almost ironic given the desire of many of them to secede from their mother country. To the extent the patriots sought unity, it was among Americans only—the unanimity of the colonies in opposing the dictates of the Crown and Parliament. And in 1776, when patriotic Americans declared independence from the patriot king, self-proclaimed patriotic factions in Parliament debated whether to support the Americans, fight them, or find some way of reaching a compromise. At some point every side in the American Revolution claimed to be patriots, with the exception of the Hessian mercenaries.

"The Last Refuge of a Scoundrel"

In any contemporary discussion of patriotism some cynic is bound to quote Samuel Johnson's aphorism, "Patriotism is the last refuge of a scoundrel." It is frequently a self-righteous indictment of patriotic sentiments, an expression that skeptics draw like a gun to offer a seemingly unanswerable retort to any patriotic appeals.[26]

But as James Boswell recorded in his diary, the circumstances of the quote were well known at the time, and Johnson's meaning was quite the opposite. On April 7, 1775, less than two weeks before shots were fired at Lexington and Concord, Boswell and Johnson were dining at a club. "Patriotism having become one of our topics," Boswell wrote, "Johnson suddenly uttered in a strong determined tone, an apophthegm, at which many will start: 'Patriotism is the last refuge of a scoundrel.'" An editorial note added, "This remarkable *sortie,* which has very much amused the world, will hereafter be still more amusing, when it is known, that it appears by the books of the club, that at the moment it was uttered *Mr. Fox was in the chair.*"[27] This refers to Charles James Fox, a radical Whig and supporter of the American cause, considered by most a political grandstander. He had adopted the term "patriot" as a means of promoting his own interests. English historian and member of Parliament Edward Gibbon observed in 1772, when Fox loudly adopted the patriot label, that he was "already attempting to pronounce the words country, liberty, corruption &c.; with what success time will discover."[28]

Samuel Johnson's true views of patriotism could not be further from his oft-quoted aphorism. In 1774 he published a long essay entitled "The Patriot" in which he critiqued what he considered the opportunistic or corrupt use of the term against a usage that owes much to Cicero. "It ought to be deeply impressed on the minds of all who have voices in this national deliberation," he wrote, "that no man can deserve a seat in parliament who is not a PATRIOT. No other man will protect our rights, no other man can merit our confidence. A *Patriot* is he whose public conduct is regulated by one single motive, the love of his country; who, as an agent in parliament, has for himself neither hope nor fear, neither kindness nor resentment, but refers every thing to the common interest."[29] In other words, scoundrels may try to pass themselves off as patriots, but no true patriot can be called a scoundrel.

The term "patriot" picked up some radical associations in the late eighteenth century, when it was associated with the excesses of the French Revolution. But patriotism generally had positive connotations in the United States, as a rallying cry and a true appeal to a beneficial form of Americanism. The word was used with increasing frequency from 1800 until the outbreak of the Civil War. It then began to decline, with temporary surges of interest during the First World War and in the 1960s. By 2000, both "patriot" and "patriotism" were being used a quarter as much as they had been 150 years earlier.[30]

The term resurged after the September 11, 2001, terrorist attacks. The brief moment of national bonding and united effort against the terror threat brought a renewed interest in the notion of patriotism. As well, the gimmicky name of the USA PATRIOT Act of

2001 guaranteed the word "patriot" would be in the forefront of the public debate.[31]

The Patriotism Gap

Surveys show that an increasing number of Americans are willing to describe themselves as patriots. A *USA Today*/Gallup poll conducted in mid-June 2010, with the Tea Party movement in full swing, showed that 32 percent of Americans described themselves as "extremely patriotic," the highest number in the reported data, up from 19 percent in 1999. The 2010 total represents an eight-point increase over the January 2002 survey, which was the first after the September 11, 2001, terrorist attacks. The most patriotic groups of Americans in the survey were self-identified Republicans and conservatives, at 52 percent and 48 percent, respectively, and those over age 65, at 40 percent. The least patriotic were self-identified Democrats and liberals (20% and 19%, respectively) and those aged 18 to 29 (22%).[32]

The most patriotic groups saw double-digit increases in "extremely" patriotic sentiment since 2005, while the least patriotic groups flat-lined or declined. When it comes to those with less patriotic fervor, among Democrats the percentages in the "somewhat" or "not especially" patriotic categories rose from 33 percent in 2005 to 37 percent, while among Republicans the number declined from 15 percent to 9 percent, with the "not especially" group being less than 0.5 percent. One reason why liberals were less willing to describe themselves as patriotic might have been that they viewed the expression as synonymous with the Tea Party movement, which in their minds was reactionary and racist.

The study noted that it was "particularly intriguing" that 42 percent of Democrats were satisfied with the direction the country is heading while a mere 7 percent of the more patriotic Republicans agreed. This 35 percent difference mirrored the 32-point patriotism gap between the two major parties. Feelings of patriotism are rarely confused with a sense of complacency. Patriotism scores declined in the early 1990s after the end of the Cold War, when the country seemed more secure and the future was less in doubt. The resurgence of patriotic sentiment reflected a measure of concern over the direction the country was taking. As with the minutemen in 1775, the patriots were responding to a call to action.

The patriotism gap broadly parallels the battle lines of the culture war. Those brought up believing the worst about the United States—the country of slavery and segregation, of unjust wars, environmental pollution, evil capitalism, and all manner of oppression—have no particular reason to be patriotic. Michelle Obama's position rang true to them when she said in February 2008 that, "for the first time in [her] adult lifetime" she was "really proud of [her] country." There was no reason *for her* to be proud of America before her husband's ascent. Likewise, candidate Barack Obama's promise to "fundamentally transform" the United States was an exciting message to those who viewed America as a morally bankrupt, internationally despised country with a despicable history. To those who hold a competing image of the United States—as a shining city on a hill; as the font of freedom; as a country of faith, hope, and charity; as the product of a divine plan; as the defender of democracy and the last best hope of mankind—the country needed no fundamental transformation.

The symbols of American history have always been available to anyone who wanted to make use of them. In the mid-1930s, the U.S. Communist Party adopted the slogan "Communism is 20th Century Americanism." It was led at the time by Earl Browder, a Kansan who did not project the image of the Bolshevik immigrant bomb thrower. The "United Front" strategy being pushed by Moscow instructed communist parties to make use of national symbols and themes to broaden their appeal. "In recent Communist thought Lincoln, Jefferson, and Tom Paine have assumed a stature comparable to that of Joseph Stalin and Vladimir Ilyich Lenin," *Time* magazine observed. "However much this may surprise the bourgeoisie, Communists planned it that way."[33] The party constitution asserted that the Communists oppose "any clique, group, circle, faction, or party, which conspires or acts to subvert, undermine, weaken or overthrow, any or all institutions of American democracy." Since this was in fact the party's goal, it showed how cynical their appeal to patriotism was.

The contemporary left bridles at the implication that they are somehow less patriotic than conservatives, regardless of what opinion polls show. Contemporary politicians of all stripes habitually seek ways to tie their legislative priorities to the touchstones of the American republic. Yet not all of them seem credible, for example when House Democratic leader Nancy Pelosi linked Obamacare directly to the Declaration of Independence. "[We] passed health care for all Americans as a right for all—not just a privilege for a few," she said in 2012, on the two-year anniversary of the law's passage. "It honored the vows of our Founders: Of life, a healthier life; liberty; the freedom to pursue our own happinesses (sic)."[34]

Critics of patriotism often scoff at its overt exhibition, such as waving flags, holding parades, or other nationalistic displays. But ceremonies can have a beneficial impact. In 2011, Andreas Madestam of Bocconi University in Italy and David Yanagizawa-Drott of Harvard's Kennedy School of Government posted findings of a study they had conducted on the impact of Independence Day celebrations on political identification and turnout. The study, "Shaping the Nation: Estimating the Impact of Fourth of July Using a Natural Experiment," found "a set of striking relationships linked to Fourth of July." According to the study, "Fourth of July celebrations have a significant impact on people's political preferences. A rain-free Fourth of July makes it 1.3 percent more likely that an individual contemporaneously identify as a Republican."[35]

The effects of the change are cumulative; the "likelihood that an adult at age 40 identifies as a Republican increases by 0.76 percentage points for each rain-free Fourth of July during childhood, where childhood is defined as the ages of 3–18." The effects are strongest at ages seven through ten, and "the estimates show that the impact on political preferences is permanent, with no evidence of the effects depreciating as individuals grow older." Unfortunately for the left, the study found "no evidence of an increased likelihood of identifying as a Democrat, indicating that Fourth of July shifts preferences to the right rather than increasing political polarization."

Attending parades in youth also can lead to greater political participation later in life. The study found that "voter turnout later in life increases by 0.62 percentage points per rain-free day" and the "likelihood that individuals attend political rallies, make campaign donations and work for political parties as adults also rises." The participation effects peak later than the preference effects, kicking in most strongly at ages 15 through 18, and tend to be less durable than the permanent pro-Republican impact.

One explanation posited by the study for these effects is that "Fourth of July is a day that provides a context for the celebration of an American civil religion organized around flags, parades and the Constitution" and that "while these values need not be partisan . . . the political right has been more successful in appropriating American patriotism and its symbols during the 20th century." Surveys released in 2010 by the Pew Research Center and Gallup support the idea that conservatives tend to consider themselves more patriotic than liberals. "According to this interpretation," the study continues, "there is a political congruence between the patriotism promoted on Fourth of July and the values associated with the Republican Party."

Conservatives did not appropriate the ideal of American patriotism; rather the left abandoned patriotism sometime in the 1960s and never came back. The liberal critique of America is dominated by multiculturalist moral relativism and victimization ideology. The former teaches that the United States and its dominant cultural currents are no better than those found elsewhere in the world, so celebrating them is a form of discrimination. The latter contends that American history is a shocking tale of slavery, exploitation, sexism, racism, imperialism, and a host of other isms. This narrative is tailored to engender a sense of entitlement in various groups that is then translated into political action and demands for special treatment. To the "blame America first" crowd, celebrating the story of the United States is simply bowing down to the dead white slave-owning elitists who stole the idea for the Constitution from the Native Americans.

But patriotism is not a thoughtless glorification of all things American, whether good or bad. It is recognition of American ideals and a belief in wanting the best for the country as a whole. It is a reaffirmation of the aspects of Americanism that speak to the best in everyone. Patriotism is a commendable sentiment, and it is only through nurturing this sense of goodness that the country can survive, if it is meant to. There is nothing wrong with the United States that couldn't be fixed if the country had more American patriots.

six

WE THE PEOPLE

In 1941 British/American journalist Alistair Cooke observed, "You cannot say too often that the United States is a nation founded on an idea, and that's what makes it unique; not on blood ties or old customs, but on an idea. The preservation of that idea, republican democracy, is the only form of unity America has known."[1] The American Constitution has been the focus and centerpiece of that unity, the foundation document that established and has preserved the republic. In a 1999 Pew Research Center poll asking why America was successful in the twentieth century, the number one answer was the Constitution, mentioned by 85 percent of respondents.

The Constitution is an expression of the American character, but it has also been used to suppress it. It is not just a document, but a system based on interpretation, case law, precedent, and tradition. Courts have recognized extensive governmental powers that are not mentioned anywhere in the document, and the part of the Constitution that best expresses American ideals, the preamble, has never been read into the case law, and officially might as well not exist.

A 2010 survey on the relevance of this Enlightenment-era document in the twenty-first century found that 54 percent of Americans said the Constitution is still effective today, against 30 percent who said it was not as effective as when it was written. Furthermore, 68 percent said the government is working worse than the way the framers intended, while only 10 percent contended it is working better.[2] The Constitution and the courts are still held in higher regard than the rest of the government, but as with other federal institutions, the general trend is downward. The document has come a long way from Philadelphia in 1787.

The Founding Fathers

The Founding Fathers were an extraordinary collection of political leaders from one of the most politicized generations in history. They and the leaders of the various state legislatures were successful because they were experienced pols, not fringe characters who seized power in a crisis or academic philosophers dreaming up an abstract utopia. They were not the rabble, they were not from the universities, they were not outsiders. They were the political elite that was part of the ruling class before, during, and after the Revolution. They understood America and its people; they knew what worked and what didn't. They had authentic legitimacy, rooted in the communities from which they came.

Progressive historian Charles A. Bead's 1913 book *An Economic Interpretation of the Constitution of the United States* influenced generations of scholars to view the Constitutional Convention as a counterrevolution in which the landed wealthy and mercantile interests conspired to impose a government that would support their interests at the expense of farmers, workers, debtors, and the common person in general. This conspiratorial view of the founding is still popular in some academic circles, particularly when linked to the critique of some of the founders as slave owners seeking to use the process to defend the "peculiar institution." But the Constitution was not the result of a coup or conspiracy; it was not imposed on an unwilling country by a secret vote. After it was drafted it was submitted to the states for ratification by elected delegates at ratification conventions. It took seven months of vigorous debates for the required nine states to ratify the document, and after twelve states ratified, Rhode Island held out for several more years.[3] But even those who objected most strongly to the Constitution went along with it in the end—they did not let the perfect destroy the good.

The Constitution erected a limited government partly because its authors rightly viewed unchecked power as the antithesis to freedom, and partly because the document was the product of compromise. Every aspect of the Constitution reflects a general mistrust of centralized authority. The form of government it established honored the varied interests of the states, the national government, and the people. The genius of the design is in the system of overlapping powers, of checks and balances that institutionalized compromise as a moderating force in government. The founders were wary of too much power being concentrated either in a particular branch of government or at the national level, and their plan sought to mitigate this whenever possible. The system is anything but efficient—that was the point. The plan was to have a cumbersome apparatus in which ambition checked ambition and the only way to get anything done was through making deals.

The Bill of Rights, the first ten amendments added to the new Constitution, was also the product of politics. They were a series of explicit guarantees that were necessary to sway enough of the opponents of the Constitution to the positive column to get the document ratified. The first five words of the First Amendment sum up the purpose of the Bill of Rights: "Congress shall make no law . . ."[4] It was the people's instruction to the federal government: "Thou shalt not." Hence the importance of the Ninth and Tenth Amendments, which sought to restate the fact that the people and states were the source and repository of rights, though later courts for the most part read these amendments out of the document.

The founders did not resolve every outstanding issue. They could not agree on a specific definition of the relationship between the states and the federal government, and they did not deal definitively with the issue of slavery. They chose to let future generations address those thorny questions, which were to dominate American politics for the next seventy plus years. It took the largest, most destructive war of the nineteenth century, with the most American dead of any conflict ever, to start to bring clarity to the problems that the founders had kicked down the road.

The Constitution set up a fight; it established an arena for conflict. It was not a utopian document listing the conditions of life for which the nation was to strive, like so many contemporary constitutions that promise jobs, housing, education, and other benefits. It simply set the rules for the continually evolving political contest that would determine how the country and its parts would be run.

The Constitution and its origins have been depoliticized and elevated in a way that diminishes the document essence as a compromise forged from one of the most dynamic and remarkable political debates in human history. Appeals to what the founders believed, wanted, or expected are limited by the fact that none of them got exactly what they wanted and all of them made compromises to settle on the final product. Every word, every aspect of the Constitution, was hashed over at the federal convention, at state conventions, and in public debate. This does not mean that there is no wisdom to be found in examining the views of the founders or those who opposed them, or that they can be ignored. In fact, studying the history of the founding produces a deep understanding of the American freedoms that the architects of the Constitution were striving to preserve.

However, seeking specific policy guidance today from original intent can be difficult. From the start, the founders had their own disputes. For example, the division between the Federalist Party and the Democratic-Republicans was deep and abiding, and Alexander Hamilton and James Madison, who coauthored the Federalist Papers and did so much to craft the Constitution, wound up on opposite sides of the divide.

The Alien and Sedition Acts, passed by the Federalist-dominated Congress in 1798, ostensibly to protect the country from the contagion of the French Revolution, were in fact aimed at shutting down the opposition press and suppressing the Democratic-Republicans. Hamilton believed the laws would promote "national unanimity," though why he felt this was necessary was unclear. In response, Madison and then–Vice President Thomas Jefferson secretly wrote and promoted the Virginia and Kentucky Resolutions, which asserted that the Alien and Sedition Acts were unconstitutional and that states had the right to take collective action against the unjust imposition of federal power.

The dispute was eventually resolved, and Jefferson's party prevailed in the 1800 elections. But the point is that if Hamilton and Madison could interpret the powers granted under the Constitution so differently just a few years after they had helped write it, seeking precise interpretive guidance from either or both of them today becomes problematic. Hamilton later lamented that "Perhaps no man in the U[nited] States has sacrificed or done more for the present Constitution than myself," and he was "labouring to prop the frail and worthless fabric" to little avail. "Every day proves to me more and more," he wrote, "that this American world was not made for me."[5]

The Use and Abuse of Judicial Review

As the Constitution was put into operation, questions arose over ambiguities in the document and the scope of laws, and it fell to the courts to settle them. The practice of judicial review, which was not stipulated in the Constitution, was never seriously questioned. The logic of judicial review was laid out by Chief Justice John Marshall in *Marbury v. Madison* (1803), although it was first used in *Hylton v. U.S.* (1796). Daniel Hylton challenged a federal law levying a sixteen-dollar fee on carriages as an unconstitutional direct tax. The Supreme Court ruled against him, and in the process became the arbiter of what the fundamental law meant. (Notably, Hamilton and Madison were on either side of this issue as well.)

Americans know less about their Constitution than they should. A 1997 survey by the National Constitution Center found that 91 percent of Americans believe that the U.S. Constitution is important to them, but a third don't know the number of branches of the federal government, almost a quarter cannot name a single right guaranteed by the First Amendment, and "84 percent believe that the U.S. Constitution is the document that states that 'all men are created equal,' thus confusing it with the Declaration of Independence."[6] Spending some time reading the document helps—long time West Virginia Senator Robert Byrd was a tireless advocate for Constitutional knowledge and carried a copy with him at all times.

Republican leaders opened the 112th Congress in January 2011 with the first-ever full reading of the Constitution on the House floor. Many on the left saw this as a sign of disrespect. The *New York Times* opined that this was "a presumptuous and self-righteous act, suggesting that they alone understand the true meaning of a text that the founders wisely left open to generations of reinterpretation."[7] Of course the fact that the previous Congress could not explain the Constitutional basis (if any) for some of its major legislative acts didn't help. And partisan views of the nature of the Constitution are strongly opposed. A July 2010 survey showed that 69 percent of Republicans agreed that the "Constitution should be interpreted as literally as possible," while only 24 percent of Democrats agreed. Likewise 65 percent of Democrats said that the "Constitution should be broadly interpreted," while only 23 percent of Republicans agreed.[8]

The *Times* was right in pointing out that the Constitution can be read in many ways, for better or worse. It is not just the document itself but everything that has come of it. The words the founders wrote are unchanged, and the amendments read the same as when they were composed. But while the words have not changed, their meaning has. The Constitution encompasses all of the logic of its interpretation over time. It includes thousands of pages of court opinions and the theories behind them. The case law—that is, the collective Supreme Court opinions that explain what the Constitution means—evolves to fit changing circumstances, adapting to politics, ideology, and intellectual fashion. Thus the same document that was used to justify the "separate but equal" doctrine later mandated racial integration. The same words that prevented most federal regulation of the economy have sanctified all federal economic micromanagement since. The same document that allowed a Judeo-Christian religious culture to mesh comfortably with public life is now a weapon used to remove all traces of religion from anything remotely connected to the government.

At some point it becomes valid to ask whether a document that can be bent, shaped, reinterpreted, and twisted to legitimize whatever the Supreme Court wants really means anything at all. The Constitution cannot simply be a tool used to justify whatever the government seeks to do—witness Solicitor General Donald Verrilli Jr.'s byzantine, twisting, and contradictory arguments before the bench in March 2012 on the constitutionality of Obamacare. Nor can it be the handmaiden to the latest intellectual fad, such as the notion of reading in aspects of international law or the Koran. If the Constitution is infinitely malleable, then it protects nothing. If this is true, as Marshall wrote in *Marbury v. Madison*, "written constitutions are absurd attempts on the part of the people to limit a power in its own nature illimitable."[9]

The Constitution follows the courts, and the courts follow politics. The justices are not above the political waves, far from it; they are a critical aspect of the functioning political system. The people appointed to life terms on the federal bench mostly reflect the politics of the president who appointed them, and the composition of the Senate that gave consent. Justices are not philosopher kings; they command respect, but they are not infallible, and they frequently disagree. Yet citizens revere the institution of the Supreme Court above the elective offices. This is why the public bridled at President Franklin Roosevelt's 1937 Judicial Procedures Reform Bill, better known as the "court-packing" scheme. Even a popular president does not have the legitimacy to radically change the composition of the court to engineer favorable rulings.

The public view of the Supreme Court has sagged in recent years. A September 2000 Gallup survey showed public approval of the Supreme Court at 62 percent and disapproval at 29 percent. By September 2011, this had fallen to a 46 percent/40 percent split.[10] A Kaiser Family Foundation poll from March 2012 showed that 23 percent had a great deal or a lot of confidence in the Supreme Court, while 47 percent had only some, and 29 percent had very little or none.[11] Another poll showed strong bipartisan public support for various means of exerting more popular control over the Supreme Court, including a retirement age for justices (69%), term limits (66%), and direct election (51%).[12]

The Constitution must stand for something irreducible. The standard of original intent is not rote literalism, but an appeal to the spirit that shaped the document and to its root theory. Yet if the fundamental law, perched on the edifice of 220 years of cases and interpretation, has become the means of subverting, suppressing, or destroying the liberties that it was supposed to defend, then it has become a contradiction, and to paraphrase Justice Marshall, absurd.

The amendment process has always provided a safety valve. More than eleven thousand Constitutional amendments have been proposed in Congress, of which twenty-seven have ultimately been adopted; one of those, the Twenty-First, repealed another, the Eighteenth or Prohibition Amendment. There is also the unused right under Article V of two-thirds of the states to call a general convention to propose amendments. Roughly twenty-nine states have standing calls for a constitutional convention. Some states rescinded their calls when the number got too close to the thirty-four required; it is worth remembering that the current Constitution was formulated at what was originally a "Grand Convention" to amend the Articles of Confederation. Lawrence Lessig of the Harvard Law School, an activist for Congressional financing reform and supporter of the Occupy movement, thinks that the threat of a convention on election finance reform could motivate the legislature to take preemptive action. The idea is to have demonstrators hold mock conventions in numerous states to try to generate momentum for the real thing.[13]

But unleashing those forces would be tricky business; the states that have expressed an interest in a convention are not controlled by parties that share the Occupiers' view of the world. The delegates they would send would be much more interested in talking about the right to life and strengthening the Second Amendment than the types of concerns that fire the imaginations of drum-beating demonstrators. A new constitutional convention would be a lively and unpredictable assemblage. Both sides of the political divide discuss the matter with a combination of hope and trepidation, but whatever came out of the convention would still have to be approved in thirty-eight states before becoming the law of the land. Whether the Constitution as we know it would survive a new convention is an open question, but America surely would.

seven

THE AMERICAN DREAM

You can't discuss America without including the American dream. It is at the core of what it means to be an American; it encapsulates the spirit of optimism and potential for individual progress. America is the arena in which the dream is played out, and the result is up to each individual dreamer.

The expression "American dream" is used in so many ways by so many people it is hard to know precisely what they mean and how to measure its achievement. In the post–Second World War era, the expression became closely associated with home ownership, and politicians sought ways to promote this goal by allowing taxpayers to deduct mortgage payments and extending government backing to home loans. Late twentieth-century subprime lender and Fannie Mae pioneer Ameriquest even called itself the "proud sponsor of the American Dream." But by 2008, Ameriquest had gone out of business; its "no-document" loans and allegedly predatory lending techniques were at the center of the housing crisis that wrecked the dreams of millions.

A recent survey of the American dream by MetLife insurance company asked people to list their most important priorities. At the top of the list were financial security, having a family, and being able to meet their basic needs. Further down were a comfortable retirement, home ownership, and a successful career and marriage. But the same study also reported that people felt they could achieve the American dream without being married, having children, being wealthy, or owning a home.[1] The dream is not necessarily tied to finances; for the most part it is a dream of personal success, the meaning of which varies from person to person.

The diversity of dreams itself may be the most American aspect of the concept. The country is a land of opportunity, a place where people have the chance to improve their lives and those of their children. The dream is dynamic, not static. Historian James Truslow Adams wrote that the continuing American epic "loses all its glory without the dream."[2] And if the dream no longer exists, then in a fundamental sense America can no longer exist.[3]

The Origins of the Dream

America and dreams—hopes, aspirations, ambitions—have been tied together from the beginning. The first uses of the expression referred to the desires of those wanting to come to America, those who dreamed of freedom. They sought some form of betterment, either achievement or the chance to try. They were inspired by portrayals of the opportunities in early America, such as in Crèvecoeur's *Letters from an American Farmer*. In America, he wrote,

> *the rewards of his industry follow with equal steps the progress of his labour; his labour is founded on the basis of nature, self-interest; can it want a stronger allurement? Wives and children, who before in vain demanded of him a morsel of bread, now, fat and frolicsome, gladly help their father to clear those fields whence exuberant crops are to arise to feed and to clothe them all; without any part being claimed, either by a despotic prince,*

> *a rich abbot, or a mighty lord. . . . The American is a new man. . . . From involuntary idleness, servile dependence, penury, and useless labour, he has passed to toils of a very different nature, rewarded by ample subsistence. This is an American.*[4]

In this classic vision, America is a land of economic opportunity, a place where individuals could prosper and each generation would be able to live better than the one that came before. The American dream is not simply or even primarily a dream of great wealth, but of honorable achievement, of fair reward for hard toil. America offered the pursuit of happiness, which was more than could be said of most European states. The British mercantile system was by no means a free economy. The Crown had long established tight controls over various economic sectors, and the changes in economic thinking laid down in Adam Smith's *The Wealth of Nations* did not appear until the revolutionary year of 1776. But the natural desire to better one's condition does not require economists to instruct people in its benefits. Those who came to the New World quickly understood that in practical terms they could do as they pleased to make their lives better. The fact that they had to struggle just to survive made this necessity a virtue.

The first clear test of whether Americans would be free to pursue their individual economic destinies or be subordinated to a mercantilist-style collective master plan took place at the Plymouth Plantation.[5] The Pilgrims had much to be thankful for in 1621. They were free from the religious persecution they had known in England and could worship and live in the manner they believed God ordained. They could also be thankful for their survival. They had established themselves on the coast of Massachusetts and made it through their first year in the New World. They had managed to plant enough food to keep them through the winter, not in luxury, certainly, but without the fear of starvation that had plagued them the year before. The circumstances seemed worthy of recognition. Edward Winslow, writing on December 12, 1621, recounted that after the harvest, Governor William Bradford "sent four men on fowling, that so we might after a special manner rejoice together after we had gathered the fruits of our labors." Winslow described the festivities, during which the Pilgrims were joined by ninety Indians led by "their greatest king Massasoit."[6] They enjoyed three days of feasting and games (such as were permitted) and good fellowship.

The Pilgrims celebrated that year in peace and plenty, but there was trouble in their utopia. Since their arrival, the settlers had practiced communal agriculture, in a manner that, according to Bradford's journal, "may well evince the vanity of that conceit of Plato's and other ancients . . . that the taking away of property and bringing in community into a commonwealth would make them happy and flourishing."[7] The fields were worked in common and their products shared out according to need. There was ample theological justification—had not Jesus and his apostles lived in this manner? Would it not thereby bring the Pilgrims closer to a state of grace? Robert Cushman, a latecomer to Plymouth (he landed in November 1621), gave a lengthy sermon to the congregation about a month after he arrived on the "Sin and Danger of Self-Love." He condemned the self-seeking man, the worship of the "belly-god," the sins of pride and conceit, the pursuit of wealth and luxury. He denounced those who had gone to Virginia full of religious zeal and been reduced to "mere worldlings." All together, all for the collective, this was the route to righteousness. He explained,

> *It wonderfully encourageth men in their duties, when they see the burthen equally borne; but when some withdraw themselves and retire to their own particular ease, pleasure, or profit, what heart can men have to go on in their business? . . . Will not a few idle drones spoil the whole stock of laborious bees so one idle-belly, one murmerer, one complainer, one self-lover will weaken and dishearten a whole Colony? Great matters have*

> *been brought to pass where men have cheerfully as was one heart, hand, and shoulder, gone about it, both in wars, buildings, and plantations, but where every man seeks himself, all cometh to nothing.*[8]

Self-interest, according to Cushman, was not the way of God; rather, to be a godly man, one must "seek the good, the wealth, the profit of others."[9]

Yet, the communalism of the Pilgrims brought out the same elements of human nature that have led to the failure of other such experiments, before and since, on grand scale and small. Throughout 1622 the contradictions of communism made themselves apparent. "The young men, that were most able and fit for labour and service, did repine that they should spend their time and strength to work for other men's wives and children without any recompense," Bradford wrote. "The strong, or man of parts, had no more in division of victuals and clothes than he that was weak and not able to do a quarter the other could; this was thought injustice."[10]

Animosities grew among the Pilgrims; the social fabric of the new colony was unraveling. Bradford notes that the situation would have grown even worse had the colonists not been united by their shared beliefs. There was no Thanksgiving feast that year, and they debated throughout the winter about how best to solve their problems. They pondered how to grow more and better crops and "not still thus languish in misery." In the spring of 1623, the Pilgrims decided to abandon their communal arrangement and divide the land among them, to allow private cultivation of crops, and to let each family work the land as they saw fit. They could "set corn every man for his own particular, and in that regard trust to themselves."[11] Each family was granted a plot according to its size, and young men who were not part of a group were assigned to one.

The results were extraordinary. Bradford wrote, "This had very good success, for it made all hands very industrious, so as much more corn was planted than otherwise would have been by any means the Governor or any other could use, and saved him a great deal of trouble, and gave far better content. The women now went willingly into the field, and took their little ones with them to set corn; which before would allege weakness and inability; whom to have compelled would have been thought great tyranny and oppression."[12] Private property brought not only increased production, but also self-respect, motivation, and harmony. The community could once again function as a center for worship, free of the social divisions they had previously suffered. And Bradford believed that the new arrangement was a much more accurate reflection of the will of God, who had made men different, who gave them varying abilities that they might employ them in the manner God intended.

Over time the Puritans developed theological grounding for the belief that those who prospered were being rewarded by God for their virtue. The secularized version of the Puritan vision became the typical American outlook toward work. In the words of German economist Max Weber, it was "that attitude which, in the pursuit of a calling, strives systematically for profit for its own sake in the manner exemplified by Benjamin Franklin." Weber was referring to Franklin's writings on work and thrift, the rewards of honest labor, and the general awareness that every moment of life is an opportunity to be productive, as summed up in Franklin's aphorism, "Time is money."[13]

And though the spirit was rooted in Calvinist theology, it spread across the country without regard to religion or national origin. It encapsulated a basic understanding that those who worked would be rewarded, those with ideas were free to pursue them, and those few men of genius or entrepreneurial spirit could become rich. When Abraham Lincoln proclaimed the first national Thanksgiving holiday, he noted that despite the demands of war, the society and economy continue to expand, and flourish. "No human counsel hath devised nor hath any mortal hand worked out these great things," he said. "They are the gracious gifts of the Most High God, who, while dealing with us in anger for our sins, hath nevertheless remembered mercy."

The capitalist fits naturally in America. The free-marketeer is a rebel, a disruptor, a revolutionary, and a change agent. This has been true whether it is Thomas Edison inventing the light bulb in his parents' basement, or Steve Jobs and Steve Wozniak inventing the future of computing in Jobs' parents' garage. The sense of opportunity and freedom to invent, innovate, and profit are essential aspects of the American character. It is why other countries, also blessed with natural resources and other advantages but lacking that spirit, have not done as well. Innovative, restless, boundary-breaking entrepreneurs, traders, and businessmen helped drive the country's emergence as a great economic power.

The free market is dynamic and always has been. American history is an endless series of cycles of empires built and diminished. Companies rise and fall. Fortunes are made and lost. The ability to fail guarantees the freedom to succeed. There are no master plans, no government offices with blueprints for the future—none that will actually work anyway—just initiative, intelligence, hard work, and the opportunity to flourish. The capitalist spirit is at the vital nexus of human desire, imagination, and the will to get things done.

Yet America was never a pure, free-market paradise. The institution of slavery was definitely not an expression of the capitalist ideal. High tariffs protected nascent American industries from foreign competition. And there were state and local economic regulations that varied depending on time and place. But the United States was still the freest of any of the industrializing countries of the nineteenth and most of the twentieth centuries, and the basic ethos, that individual initiative and hard work led to just rewards, was firmly embedded in the culture. The pursuit of happiness was every American's inheritance.

The late nineteenth century was a time of major new inventions and rapid economic expansion. Social mobility became part and parcel of the dream, particularly for the millions of immigrants arriving on America's shores. "If a group has internal vitality, a will—if it has aspiration," wrote democratic socialist activist Michael Harrington, "it may live in dilapidated housing, it may eat an inadequate diet, and it may suffer poverty, but it is not impoverished. So it was in those ethnic slums of the immigrants that played such a dramatic role in the unfolding of the American dream."[14] Those who arrived in America and found themselves in difficult circumstances knew that their conditions did not define who they were. "The people found themselves in slums, but they were not slum dwellers."[15] As John Roche wrote, the immigrant "was exploited, but not alienated. He never lost his most priceless possession—his hope." And the greatest justification of American accomplishment is that "this hope, this trust in freedom, has been so grandly vindicated."[16]

Best-selling author Horatio Alger (1832–1899) became the pied piper of the American dream. He published more than one hundred books aimed chiefly at young men, telling stories in which scrappy youngsters went from rags to middle-class lives through initiative, hard work, and making the most of opportunities. Alger's tales were not about excess, not stories of becoming robber barons or falling overnight into wealth, but juvenile morality tales geared toward developing respectable members of society. It was a very different message from the type that children get from contemporary popular culture, with its emphasis on excessive wealth, celebrity, shock, and sex; achievement without hard work; and pleasure without responsibility.

Of course Alger's time had its excesses as well, as satirized in Mark Twain and Charles Dudley Warner's novel *The Gilded Age*, a farce about land speculation and influence peddling. Yet the book was not a blanket moral indictment of gain. In the preface to the 1897 London edition, Twain explained,

> *In America nearly every man has his dream, his pet scheme, whereby he is to advance himself socially or pecuniarily. It is this all-pervading speculativeness which we tried to illustrate in "The Gilded Age." It is a characteristic which is both bad and good, for both the individual and the nation. Good, because it allows neither to stand still, but drives both for ever on, towards some point or other which is ahead, not behind nor at one side. Bad, because the chosen point is often badly chosen, and then the individual is wrecked; the aggregations of such cases affects the nation, and so is bad for the nation. Still, it is a trait which is of course better for a people to have and sometimes suffer from than to be without.*[17]

The United States went through a number of economic crises in the nineteenth and early twentieth centuries, but the Great Depression became the greatest single challenge to the idea of the free economic system. Capitalism was declared a failure, and New Deal liberals stepped in with supposed government solutions to every problem. Statism was the spirit of the times at home and especially abroad. Mussolini's fascists were credited with getting the trains to run on time, even if they didn't. Nazi discipline seemed to stabilize and strengthen the moribund German economy, even as Hitler prepared for war and genocide. And Stalin reported miracles of collectivization and industrialization in the Soviet Union, which turned out simply to be lies covering up a system of oppression and state terror. Across the world, people looked to governments to solve all of their problems, only to find out that the state was composed of people with the same flaws and foibles as anyone else, but unfortunately armed with excessive power.

It was during these dark days that the expression "the American dream" came into its own. In 1933, historian James Truslow Adams published *The Epic of America*, which charted the origins and development of the American people. He popularized a definition of "the American dream, that dream of a land in which life should be richer and fuller for every man, with opportunity for each, according to his ability and achievement." According to Adams, it is "not a dream of motor cars and high wages merely, but a dream of a social order in which each man and each woman shall be able to attain to the fullest stature of which they are innately capable, and be recognized by others for what they are, regardless of the fortuitous circumstances of birth or possession."[18] The American dream reflected a belief in the goodness of common people, in their desire to achieve, their fairness, and their desire for the best for themselves, their families, and their communities. Adams' book was widely read, and it stood as a vote of confidence in uncertain times that the American spirit was strong enough to weather any hardships and emerge better, having withstood the test.

The American Nightmare

In February 1964, Dr. Martin Luther King Jr. spoke at Drew University about the American dream. "America is essentially a dream, a dream yet unfulfilled," he said, that was defined in the "amazing universalism" of the Declaration of Independence, which declares all men are created equal, with "basic rights that are neither derived from nor conferred by the state. They are gifts from the hands of the Almighty God. Very seldom if ever in the history of the world has a socio-political document expressed in such profound eloquent and unequivocal language the dignity and the worth of human personality." Dr. King believed the United States was a "schizophrenic personality, tragically divided against herself," because racial discrimination prevented the full realization of the dream. Eliminating this discrimination from American life was a morally necessary requirement for making the dream a reality for everyone.[19]

Two months later another black leader thoroughly repudiated Dr. King's vision. In one of his most noted speeches, "The Ballot or the Bullet," Malcolm X thoroughly rejected the notion of the American dream and, moreover, the idea that black people could even be Americans. He said,

> *Being here in America doesn't make you an American. Being born here in America doesn't make you an American. . . . No, I'm not an American. I'm one of the 22 million black people who are the victims of Americanism. One of the 22 million black people who are the victims of democracy, nothing but disguised hypocrisy. So, I'm not standing here speaking to you as an American, or a patriot, or a flag-saluter, or a flag-waver—no, not I. I'm speaking as a victim of this American system. And I see America through the eyes of the victim. I don't see any American dream; I see an American nightmare.*[20]

Malcolm X is sometimes credited with coining the expression "the American nightmare," but in fact it was well established by the time he began discussing it. Not everyone in America bought into the notion of the dream; this had been true since the earliest days. Free societies produce critics—this is a characteristic and strength of freedom—but among them there are always those who will see only the downside, and whose solution to America's ills is to transform the system as a whole.

Critiques of the American dream follow standard patterns. Some believe it does not exist, that it is a myth concocted to fool working people. Others believe that it is not worth pursuing, or has a negative effect on the society as a whole. Some see it promoting love of wealth over love of community and rampant consumerism over good financial sense. To these critics, the American dream either could not be attained or, if it were, would not result in the happiness that was promised. They hearken back to Robert Cushman preaching the virtues of communism in the winter of 1621 as the Pilgrims wondered how they would survive through the next year.

Open criticism of the dream is nothing new. In 1819 a Briton warned his compatriots about the downside of the vision of America as a land of milk and honey. "A kind of Americo-mania has possessed many of our countrymen," he wrote, "who seemed to think that the land flowed so abundantly with good things, that they needed only to open their mouths and let them have entrance. I need hardly say that this is a gross delusion. . . . Hundreds have come to America who bitterly lament their folly; and who have found, to their dear-bought experience, that gold neither paves the streets, nor grows upon the trees."[21]

Leftist critic Mary McCarthy noted in 1961 that "the *American Nightmare* is a prime domestic topic. If the heroic image is cherished by Americans, the villainous image has not been neglected. There is no anti-Americanism as eloquent as that of the native American."[22] In fact, some of the most influential literature of the twentieth century sought to disparage the American dream. Upton Sinclair's 1906 propagandistic novel *The Jungle* purported to be a fact-based account of the hopeless lives of American immigrants and the horrifying conditions of the meatpacking industry. F. Scott Fitzgerald's *The Great Gatsby* portrayed the corrupting influences of material success and its pursuit on the values that gave the American dream substance. It was an indictment of the life of the wealthy during the Roaring Twenties, with its vulgarity, ostentation, and lack of moral fiber. John Steinbeck's award-winning 1939 novel *The Grapes of Wrath* was a critique of the American dream during the Great Depression whose overriding theme was the futility of effort. Arthur Miller's award-winning 1949 play *Death of a Salesman* presented a bleak take on various aspects of the American dream, with no happy endings.

American author Henry Miller was a persistent critic of American consumerism and provincialism. In *The Air Conditioned Nightmare*, an account based on his experiences during a road trip through America from 1939 to 1941, he penned a comprehensive critique of the American self-image:

> *We are accustomed to think of ourselves as an emancipated people; we say that we are democratic, liberty-loving, free of prejudices and hatreds. This is the melting-pot, the seat of a great human experiment. Beautiful words, full of noble, idealistic sentiment. Actually we are a vulgar, pushing mob whose passions are easily mobilized by demagogues, newspaper men, religious quacks, agitators and such like. To call this a society of free peoples is blasphemous. What have we to offer the world besides the superabundant loot which we recklessly plunder from the earth under the maniacal delusion that this insane activity represents progress and enlightenment?*[23]

But even by mid-century, when Henry Miller was writing, this critique was neither shocking nor original. Intellectuals of various stripes—Marxists, socialists, anarchists, populists, progressives, and a variety of others—had spread this account of the American dream so widely that it was passé. In his review of Miller's book, novelist and critic Isaac Rosenfeld observed that the "America of the glaring contrasts, of riches and poverty and tons of food wasted, has become a household notion. The American nightmare has taken the place of the American dream, and it is as sentimental as its predecessor, as popular and as widely believed in. We all know our shame and our disgrace by now; they have blended with the breakfast coffee."[24] By the time the New Left radicals of the 1960s came around, they were simply recycling themes that were already stale when they were born. Nevertheless, they believed that fashionable cynicism, like sex, began with their generation.

Some blamed America for having achieved the dream. John Kenneth Galbraith's influential 1958 book *The Affluent Society* affirmed that American capitalism had produced an over-abundantly wealthy country in which most people had everything they needed. It was time, he believed, to enter a new phase, to raise taxes, enlarge the government—euphemistically known as the "public sector"—end poverty, and promote a new vision of a society of limits.[25] In his 1962 book, *The Other America,* Michael Harrington claimed that the old view of the American dream was no longer operative because those mired in the "new poverty" could not get out. These ideas were at the root of Lyndon Johnson's plan to build a Great Society and brought the country the War on Poverty, urban renewal, and a host of government social programs intended to alleviate these perceived ills. At the time, the United States was by most measures at the height of its global power and influence and arguably could afford to dabble in these social experiments. But such entitlements have since grown to dominate federal budgets and drive the trillion-dollar deficits that make future economic prosperity doubtful, particularly as America struggles against a rise in foreign economic competitors.

The poor, of course, are still with us. Bureau of the Census figures show that the number of Americans in poverty has been more than 30 million for the last two decades. But the official definition of poverty is far from what most people would consider destitution. A recent report from the Heritage Foundation based on census data and other government surveys showed that "the typical household defined as poor by the government had a car and air conditioning. For entertainment, the household had two color televisions, cable or satellite TV, a DVD player, and a VCR. If there were children, especially boys, in the home, the family had a game system, such as an Xbox or a PlayStation. In the kitchen, the household had a refrigerator, an oven and stove, and a microwave. Other household conveniences included a clothes washer, clothes dryer, ceiling fans, a cordless phone, and a coffee maker. The home of the typical poor family was not overcrowded and was in good repair. In fact, the typical poor American had more living space than the average European."[26] Granted there is more to the American dream than a color television and a ceiling fan, and some Americans live in genuinely dire circumstances. But it says much about American perceptions of poverty that people are said to be disadvantaged who have a standard of living greater than that of 90 percent of the rest of the world.

Critiquing the American dream is good business; filmmaker Michael Moore has made a fortune on it. While his estimated worth is more than $50 million, he claims that he is not wealthy because he fights for the poor. "That's how I spend my time, my energy, my money," he said, "on trying to upend this system that I think is a system of violence, it's a system that's unfair to the average working person of this country."[27] He claimed that the assets of the wealthy are actually up for grabs. "That's not theirs," he said, "that's a national resource, that's ours. We all have this—we all benefit from this or we all suffer as a result of not having it."[28] Presumably, those suffering include people kept out of Mr. Moore's sprawling vacation home on exclusive Torch Lake in Michigan.

Left-wing activist Anthony Kapel "Van" Jones has actively tried to appropriate the rhetoric of the American dream. He denounces the "dream killers," principally the rich, "who are not working that hard at all," and are making life hard for lower-income Americans, "people who are working the hardest and following the rules . . . the ones who are being left behind." There are "two American dreams." He says:

> *One of them I call the "American fantasy." You know that one? Everyone is going to be rich. Everybody. And we're all going to be able to ride out to the great white suburbs, get a McMansion,*

> *get flat-screened TVs to cover up the holes in our lives. That is the American fantasy, which is turning out to be the American nightmare. It is dying out on its own accord—it deserves no defense and it will get no defense.*[29]

In 2011, Jones cosponsored the Rebuild the Dream campaign as an explicit counter to the Tea Party movement. He announced the "Contract for the American Dream," which included familiar big government–oriented planks such as creating "green" jobs, raising taxes on the rich, cutting defense budgets, increasing government education spending, and sponsoring infrastructure projects. This version of the American dream does not seek greater opportunities so much as guaranteed payments. It replaces the pursuit of happiness with the receipt of state assistance. To Jones, the American dream is just a bigger government handout, paid for by the efforts of others.

President Obama has also been obsessed with the dream. The subtitle of his 2006 book the *The Audacity of Hope* is *Thoughts on Reclaiming the American Dream*, and he works the expression into every speech he can. But his view of the dream is similar to Jones' in that he believes that the dream cannot be achieved without government action. He said the government needs to be "fighting for working people day in and day out, making sure that we are trying to allow them to live out the American dream."[30] For Mr. Obama, the pursuit of happiness requires government permission.

The most concerted attacks on the dream come from activists obsessed with the environment. Their rallying cries—global climate change, global warming, global weirding—seek to make the case for increased government regulation and centralized control of economic activity to forestall a predicted environmental catastrophe. They try to harness guilt, blaming Americans for their affluence and their "unsustainable" lifestyles, and demanding that they radically reduce their "carbon footprint" to save the planet. But an MIT study from 2008 found that even the lifestyle of an American homeless person or Buddhist monk generates carbon dioxide emissions that are double the global average and well above what the United Nations seeks to mandate for all humanity.[31]

Even the venerable tradition of Thanksgiving has come under attack from those who think that Americans simply have too much.[32] It is now commonplace in November to hear calls for making the holiday "eco-friendly" and "sustainable." To the left, Thanksgiving is steeped in sin. It has long been politically incorrect to liberals, who see it as a celebration of the European invasion of North America. The day is known as "thanks-taking" to American Indian activists. And in recent years Thanksgiving has also become an affront to the environmental movement. It is the day when Americans' carbon footprints grow three sizes as they travel long distances to feast on factory-fed turkeys and consume far too much electricity watching football on TV. The answer, the environmentalists preach, is to cut back. Don't travel. Eat less, and sustainably. Take walks instead of watching bowl games.

The notion of a "sustainable Thanksgiving" has more than a whiff of yuppiedom about it. The movement was created by and for those who can afford to choose expensive alternatives such as locally grown organic food and designer turkeys. These are people who look forward to pointing out to their guests how virtuous they are because they are burning soy-based candles and composting their vegetable peelings.

"The New England colonists never intended for Thanksgiving to be a day of gluttony," author Elyssa East sniffed in the *New York Times*.[33] Truly, gluttony is a vice, but Thanksgiving is a celebration of the virtues that made the plenty possible. It should be celebrated in a spirit of hope, faith, and optimism. Thanksgiving is a time to acknowledge and rejoice in the blessings of being American. It is the holiday during which friends and family gather to renew the bonds of harmony and honor our Creator for the joys of life. The notion of a sustainable Thanksgiving is at odds with the spirit of the holiday. We are not giving thanks for limits, but for abundance. Especially in times of relative want, it is important to recognize and celebrate the blessings of our country. Thanksgiving and sustainability cannot coexist. Everything about Thanksgiving is unsustainable by design: the traveling, the feasting, the football, the Macy's Thanksgiving Day Parade. The most sustainable Thanksgiving would be none at all.

The Fading Dream

The American dream has come under such persistent attack that there is an understandable undercurrent of pessimism about it. In May 2011, Gallup.com posted an article under the headline, "Optimism About Future for Youth Reaches All-Time Low." According to Gallup, "Forty-four percent of Americans believe it is likely that today's youth will have a better life than their parents, even fewer than said so amid the 2008–2009 recession, and the lowest on record for a trend dating to 1983." Fifty-five percent thought it unlikely or very unlikely that young people would have a better life, and only 13 percent thought it was very likely that things would be better. These numbers are even lower than those reported in December 2008 in the midst of the economic meltdown. The report concluded that "confidence in the traditional American dream—that each generation can work its way up in the world and have a better life than the previous generation—appears to be slipping away."[34]

Other polls reflect this disturbing downward trend. A November 2010 Associated Press/CNBC poll asked, "Do you expect that life for the next generation of Americans will be better than life today, worse than life today, or about the same as life today?" Only 21 percent thought life would be better, 33 percent the same, and 45 percent believed things would be worse.[35] CBS News periodically asks the question, "Do you think the future of the next generation of Americans will be better, worse, or about the same as life today?" In June 2000 the response was 40 percent better, 31 percent worse, and 26 percent the same. By May 2010 the "better" response was cut in half to 20 percent, "worse" had risen to 50 percent, and "the same" stayed about the same.[36]

Another poll showed that even current generations are starting to feel that maybe they have not done better than their parents. CBS News asked, "Compared to your parents' generation, do you think in general your opportunities to succeed in life are better than theirs, about the same as theirs, or worse than theirs?" In February 2000, 72 percent were certain that opportunities were better, and a mere 5 percent thought they were worse. By December 2009, the "worse" figure had swollen to 27 percent, and those thinking opportunities were better had dropped sharply to 47 percent.[37] A July 2011 Zogby poll showed that 50 percent of Americans believed that it was possible to achieve the American dream, while the other half was either not sure or said the dream did not exist. But believers in the dream had dropped 18 percent since the November 2008 election.[38]

One of the predominant themes of the Occupy movement is the frustration some young people feel at having been promised something that they feel is being denied them. Youth unemployment is high, and to many young people the future does not look promising. In the fall of 2011, one Occupier posted, "When I was younger and my dad would ask what I wanted to be when I grew up. I always said 'happy' and he would always retort with 'you don't understand how things work, you're still too young.' But, what he didn't realize was that it didn't matter what I wanted to be anyway because by the time I was 'old enough to understand' and old enough for college I would have to work more hours than were in a day to pay for an unsatisfactory education or be put into debt for the rest of my life. What he didn't understand was that I would be lucky to be happy when I grew up. What he didn't understand was that being happy is the new American dream, because the old one was a sham." "I followed the American Dream and feel like I got scammed," said another. "It's only the American dream if you're asleep," wrote a third.[39]

Some Occupiers wanted to make enabling the "pursuit of happiness" a government function. One of the movement's major working documents proposed that the government "should be held accountable for achieving specific Gross National Happiness [GNH] index target values." The notion of a gross national happiness index was pioneered by the country of Bhutan, which conducts an annual assessment of national happiness based on a series of metrics measuring health, well-being, and good governance. Proposed policies have to pass a GNH review and require a GNH impact statement. Some American activists have begun to celebrate "National Pursuit of Happiness Day" on April 13, Thomas Jefferson's birthday. But subjecting the concept of happiness to measurement, monitoring, and enforcement by the government is counterintuitive. It is not in the nature of the state to produce happiness. The bureaucratization of joy will surely lead down some dark and contradictory roads, particularly when individual notions of the pursuit of happiness clash with government mandates. The last thing the American people need is for Washington to make the same contribution to "gross national happiness" that government-backed mortgages did to the housing market.

Restoring the Dream

But regardless of the general air of pessimism, some studies show a ray of hope. The March 2011 study by Xavier University's Center for the Study of the American Dream found interesting, mixed results. The study showed that two-thirds of Americans said that things have gone on the wrong track in the country, only 41 percent expected the economy to get better in 2012, and a scant 23 percent felt that America was on the rise. However, despite these gloomy prognostications, individual belief in the American dream remained strong. Sixty-three percent of the respondents were either very or extremely confident that they would be able to reach the American dream in their lifetimes.[40] This shows that the dream speaks to the American faith in individual achievement; regardless of a sluggish economy or even the belief that things may get worse overall, individuals can still achieve their dreams through applied effort.

The American dream is not owning a house, becoming wealthy, or having the government give you a job. The American dream is not determined by an opinion poll or a government happiness survey; it is not distributed like proverbial loaves of bread at the Roman circus, or bestowed out of the generosity of all-wise political leaders. The dream is an idea, the notion that through individual effort everyone in America has an opportunity to get ahead. The type of effort, and what it means to succeed, are left to each person to decide. But like all dreams, it exists in the minds and visions of the American people. It is something more than a mere hope; it is a personal standard against which to judge one's life and accomplishments. It is the opportunity to be able to say, "Today, I am living the dream."

eight

COMING TO AMERICA

America is a nation of immigrants. It is the beneficiary of the most significant migration in human history, which unleashed the creative energies of millions of people and created an unprecedented, dynamic society. Being a nation of immigrants is not just a historical fact, but a core characteristic of Americanism. It reinforces the notion that America is more an idea than a place. Anyone can be an American, if they choose to be one.

Historically, immigration and the American dream are tightly linked. People have emigrated for many reasons—to flee war or persecution, to seek economic opportunity, to worship in the manner of their choosing, or simply to escape the social, familial, or other bonds of their old lives and reinvent themselves—but all are tied to the aspiration to have a better life for oneself and one's family. And although America is a nation of immigrants, it is not a country where people came in order to remain immigrants. The United States was a place people could come to leave their old lives behind and meld into the American culture. And those who chose to land on America's shores one hundred or more years ago went out of their way to show love for their adopted country.

Yet immigration has been a controversial issue, and it remains so today. The number of people coming to America is reaching new levels. Illegal immigrants cross the lightly protected borders, and while the Obama administration brags about record numbers of deportations, the Justice Department is suing frontline states trying to get the situation under control. Cities declare themselves sanctuaries even as they cannot pay for the social services required by their citizens. Multiculturalists cheer the changing ethnic composition of the country while maintaining that newcomers should not integrate but maintain and strengthen their separate identities. The melting pot has turned into a pressure cooker.

The First New Nation

"What then is the American, this new man?" wrote Crèvecoeur in his *Letters from an American Farmer.* He answers the question thus:

> *He is either a European, or the descendant of a European, hence that strange mixture of blood, which you will find in no other country. I could point out to you a family whose grandfather was an Englishman, whose wife was Dutch, whose son married a French woman, and whose present four sons have now four wives of different nations. He is an American, who leaving behind him all his ancient prejudices and manners, receives new ones from the new mode of life he has embraced, the new government he obeys, and the new rank he holds. He becomes an American by being received in the broad lap of our great Alma Mater. Here individuals of all nations are melted into a new race of men, whose labours and posterity will one day cause great changes in the world. Americans are the western pilgrims, who are carrying along with them that great mass of arts, sciences, vigour, and industry which began long since in the east; they will finish the great circle.*[1]

Immigration is a story as old as Jamestown. It is as old as St. Augustine, Florida, founded by the Spanish in 1565. With respect to the peoples who arrived in successive waves across the Bering Strait, it is thousands of years older, and if the controversial Solutrean hypothesis is correct, the first peoples from what is now Europe arrived even earlier, up to twenty-one thousand years ago.[2]

A British traveler in America in 1806 wrote that immigration "forms a wonderful feature in the American character. . . . With a large and liberal policy we welcome every alien. And if to live under a Government anxious to do justice and to preserve peace, to be subject to no other will than that of the majority, to have the profits of his labour secure, and his right of opinion fully admitted, will add to his happiness, here the emigrant may be happy."[3] Immigrants are voluntary participants in the American experiment, and the true claim for the country to be the empire of liberty is that it is composed of those who chose to join it. In 1848, Senator Daniel Dickinson of New York, waxing on the expansion of the country following the war with Mexico, spoke of "the sound of the pattering feet of coming millions" and saw "races to civilize, educate and absorb—as America's triumph in the cause of progress and civilization" continued.[4]

At that time the country was in the midst of its largest of several waves of Irish immigration. The great potato famine of 1845–1852 drove hundreds of thousands to seek a new life in America.[5] These immigrants were generally very poor and the conditions under which they made the passage were terrible, with perhaps 40 percent succumbing to disease. There was some anti-Irish prejudice among nativists, and "No Irish need apply" was a common appendix to want ads. Political groups such as the Know-Nothing Party exploited anti-immigrant and anti-Catholic feelings, but they never gained widespread support and soon faded. And the Irish came with some advantages; they spoke English, knew politics, and became a link between the polity and non-English speaking Catholics from Germany and later Italy. They were well organized, especially in the cities, and eventually began to dominate civic offices and the church hierarchy where they were concentrated. Irish participation in the Civil War, such as in the Union Army's "Irish Brigade," which was made up of regiments of recruits primarily of Irish heritage, also gave the Sons of Erin a claim on America.

After the Civil War, railroads played an important role in bringing people to America. The large land grants given to the railroad companies were contingent on bringing settlers to the land, and the easiest way to do this was to find people overseas. Railroad companies had recruiting agents throughout Europe, particularly in the central and eastern countries and in Scandinavia. Rapid industrialization in the United States also increased demand for workers, and immigrants met it in the growing industrial centers of the Midwest and the Great Lakes region. Advancements in shipping made the journey to the New World relatively safer, speedier, and less expensive.

Many European states were happy to see the migrants go. The population boom was on, and in 1798 English economist Thomas Malthus had predicted that some time in the middle of the nineteenth century world population would outrun the food supply. It was one of the most noted and influential—and ultimately erroneous—predictions of catastrophic scarcity in history, and made "Malthusian" a watchword for mistaken alarmism. Yet many in Europe believed that the departure of the "surplus population" for America would be beneficial. There were few emigration restrictions, and if people could afford to leave, they should do so.[6]

The result was that through self-selection the people with the most drive, imagination, and determination to better their lives took the opportunity to make the journey to America, depriving their home countries of their energies and abilities. It was not exactly what would later be called a "brain drain," but America was a magnet for people of drive and ambition. And for many Europeans the pull factors were enormous; the quality of life, even in an American slum, was often well above what they were used to in their countries of origin.

The Road to Ellis Island

For decades there were no firm rules governing immigration to America. People showed up, one way or another, and simply became part of the colonial experiment. In 1740 the British Parliament passed "An Act for Naturalizing such foreign Protestants, and others therein mentioned, as are settled or shall settle in any of His Majesty's Colonies in America." The act extended full citizenship to any covered by the law who had lived in America for seven years, provided they took an oath to the Crown and could prove they had taken the Sacrament. The act also applied to Jews who took a modified oath that omitted references to Christianity.

Starting with the Revolution, naturalization was left primarily to the states, with some exceptions. In 1778 the Articles of Confederation conferred blanket citizenship on everyone in the rebelling states (which was also a way of establishing legally that anyone who didn't back the Revolution was a traitor). A series of laws passed by Congress in the 1790s imposed residency requirements for naturalization eligibility of first two years (1790), then five years (1795), then fourteen years (1798). These acts were both an attempt to shut out potential mass migration of Europeans radicalized by the French Revolution and a reflection of domestic political struggles between the Federalists and Jeffersonians. In 1802 during Jefferson's presidency, the residency requirement was reduced back to five years, but there was no standardized system of recording or enforcing citizenship for another century. The matter was primarily left to states or even localities. Given the spotty record keeping of the time, variations in local requirements, the number of immigrants arriving, and their movement across the country, the definition of who was a citizen was at times subjective. Children became naturalized with their parents, wives were naturalized with their husbands (prior to 1922), and people in territories acquired by the United States were usually given automatic citizenship. In addition, service in the military became a speedy route to citizenship after 1862.

Although immigration and citizenship were national responsibilities, the states had a recognized interest in the process. This interest was established in 1837 by the Supreme Court in *New York v. Miln,* when it upheld a New York law that required immigrants to register with the city of New York and held shipmasters financially responsible with respect to any passenger "to indemnify and save harmless" the city "from all expenses of the maintenance of such person or of the child or children of such person born after such importation." The Supreme Court ruled that these measures fell under the state's police powers, and were "intended to prevent the state's being burdened with an influx of foreigners and to prevent their becoming paupers, and who would be chargeable as such." Since "the end and means here used are within the competency of the states," the law was upheld.

The immigration process was not truly nationalized until Congress passed the Immigration Act of 1891, creating the Bureau of Immigration and Naturalization. Federal officials registered immigrants at ports of entry, the most noted station being on Ellis Island in New York Harbor; between 1892 and 1954 it processed twelve million future citizens. The nearby Statue of Liberty was dedicated six years before the Ellis Island station began operating. The statue was not originally intended to be a symbol of immigration, but Emma Lazarus' poem "The New Colossus," written for a fundraiser for the statue's pedestal, solidified Lady Liberty's symbolic role in welcoming newcomers to America:

"Keep, ancient lands, your storied pomp!" cries she
With silent lips. "Give me your tired, your poor,

Your huddled masses yearning to breathe free,
The wretched refuse of your teeming shore.
Send these, the homeless, tempest-tost to me,
I lift my lamp beside the golden door!"

The poem neatly strikes the themes that defined the country and its promise: a rejection of the constraints of the Old World, a belief in the potential of the common person, and the dignity of living free in the country of one's choice. Indeed liberty is an apt symbol for immigration, since it involves the fundamental choice to live, and to live in America.

Slamming the Golden Door

There have always been those who wanted to keep immigrants out, to close the golden door after their ancestors were safely inside. This was true from the country's earliest days. John Adams argued against granting a visa to French economist Pierre Samuel du Pont de Nemours in 1798, saying "we have had too many French philosophers already."[7] Du Pont managed to emigrate to Delaware the following year anyway. His son, chemist E. I. du Pont, began producing gunpowder there in 1804 and founded what is now one of the largest chemical companies in the world.

Nativist sentiment usually accompanied large influxes of new arrivals. It reappeared in the late nineteenth century with the surge of immigrants from southern Europe, Italy, Greece, and the Balkans, and Slavs and Jews from the Pale of Settlement in the east. Labor groups, some of which were dominated by previous waves of immigrants, saw these newcomers as a threat to their jobs. Others appealed to racial theories, which at the time were generally accepted as the cutting edge of human science. Social Darwinism and other concepts were used to justify limits as to who might mix with the American social body.

Asians, being more culturally removed and different in appearance from the Europeans, felt the first official limits. The Chinese Exclusion Act of 1882 was a response to what alarmists called the "yellow peril." The argument was that people from Asia were so unlike the rest of the country that they were unassimilable and therefore had to be kept out to preserve the essential nature of the polity. It was the type of argument that had been made in some quarters regarding previous immigrant groups and has been made since. A sarcastic column on the issue from 1913 resonates a century later with the contemporary immigration debate:

> *[San Francisco] Mayor Phelan says that [the Japanese] menace lies in the fact that "they are skilled agriculturists and unassimilable." I don't know what menace to society there may be in a man's being a skilled agriculturist. But if there is such a menace it might be well to begin on this reform by wiping out forty or fifty American colleges of agriculture and going back to the old unskilled grandfather way of robbing the land this year and letting next year look out for itself. As to the matter of assimilation of foreigners—this has been an American nightmare ever since the day when the "Know-Nothing" Party thought the Irish were unassimilable. Since that day we have made good American citizens out of unassimilable dagoes, Sheenies and Greasers. Possibly we shall do as well with the Japs if we have patience. . . . If it is necessary to have a plague of Orientals in order to restrain the American farmer from working himself to death, let us have it soon and plenty. Maybe the Japanese are unassimilable. But I have seen some of their women who look a good sight more assimilable than some American women I might name.*[8]

The people who have raised the banner of Americanism as a means of keeping out those who want to become citizens legitimately contradict a fundamental tenet of the cause that they claim to champion. The American spirit does not countenance denying others the opportunity to seek the same freedoms and opportunities that define the character of the country. And it might be shocking to the believers in the "yellow peril," as well as the contemporary multiculturalists who champion the Asians as oppressed people, to learn that Asian-Americans make up the top median income group, with family incomes 25 percent higher than the national average.

America the Melting Pot

Assimilation, the fertile union of many peoples, has always been a core strength of the country. Each group contributes national characteristics that add to the overall quality of life. An English visitor in 1804 noted the diversity of manners in the United States, derived from "the continual influx of a vast number of foreigners," such as the "frugality and plainness of the High and Low Dutch, the industry and parsimony of the Scots, the genius, conviviality, and want of economy of the English, the hardiness of the Irish, who are of the lower order, and the frivolity of the French." Yet "they all, sooner or later, give way to the general mass of American customs, which long usage and republican genius have established."[9] In 1814, then–New York City Mayor DeWitt Clinton praised the beneficial effects of the multinational character of America. "Perhaps our mingled descent from various nations may have a benign influence upon genius," he wrote. "The extraordinary characters which the United States have produced may be, in some measure, ascribed to the mixed blood of so many nations flowing in our veins."[10]

From the start there has been no official assimilation process, no government procedure other than the varied citizenship requirements. Assimilation came largely through immersion, and it worked. People adapted to life in America as a natural consequence of wanting to be here. They did not come as immigrants to remain immigrants, they came to build lives as Americans. Ethnic enclaves in cities rose and fell and were replaced by other groups as the earlier waves integrated into the society at large, leaving behind place names and restaurants. Children born in the United States to immigrant parents quickly adopted the culture of the country, because it was in fact their country. Schools that taught in native languages without government subsidy folded over time as demand dried up. The same was true of foreign language newspapers that first flourished, then receded. People wanted to learn English, and the culture encouraged them to do so. Coming to America meant making the effort to be an American.

The ideal of assimilation was summed up in the expression "the melting pot," which was popularized by an early twentieth-century play of the same name by Israel Zangwill, a British writer and son of Jewish immigrants from Latvia and Poland. The play was a rousing dramatization of American immigration that invoked imagery of the fusion of peoples in this country and echoed previous generations' belief in America as part of an unfolding divine plan.

> *There she lies, the great Melting Pot. Listen! Can't you hear the roaring and the bubbling? There gapes her mouth—the harbor where a thousand mammoth feeders come from the ends of the world to pour in their human freight. Ah, what a stirring and a seething! Celt and Latin, Slav and Teuton, Greek and Syrian—black and yellow. Yes, East and West, and North and South, the palm and the pine, the pole and the equator, the crescent and the cross—how the great Alchemist melts and fuses them with his purging flame! Here shall they all unite to build the Republic of Man and the kingdom of God. Ah, what is the glory of Rome and Jerusalem where all nations and races come to worship and look back, compared with the glory of America, where all races come to labor and look forward.*[11]

The New World was indeed forward looking, not bound by the petty, timeless, irresolvable disputes that wracked the rest of the world. America was a new creation, a clean slate, where people left behind their ancient struggles. The romantically named hero of *The Melting Pot,* David Quixano, who emigrates after his family is killed in a pogrom, declares that "America is God's crucible." He addressed the immigrants at Ellis Island who arrived "in your fifty groups, with your fifty languages and your histories and your fifty blood feuds and rivalries." But they were to abandon the past, because "these are the fires of God! A fig for your feuds and vendettas! Germans and Frenchmen, Irishmen and Englishmen, Jews and Russians—into the crucible with you all! God is making the American." And in fact the United States has been remarkably free of echoes of ethnic and national conflicts abroad. The sectarian and national struggles of Europe, Asia, and the Mideast were settled at the dinner tables and in the bedrooms of America.

The Melting Pot was a popular hit of the 1908–1909 theater season and was acclaimed as a masterpiece and the great American play, even though—or particularly because—it was written by a British Jew of East European extraction. However, not everyone lauded it; a *New York Times* reviewer opined, "'The Melting Pot' is sentimental trash masquerading as a human document. That is the sum and substance of it."[12] But after the opening in Washington, D.C., in October 1909, Theodore Roosevelt shouted from his box, "That's a great play, Mr. Zangwill, that's a great play."[13]

Roosevelt, who had left the White House the previous March, was president during the peak years of the immigration wave at the turn of the century. His record on the issue was mixed—for example, he fought to end Japanese segregation in California schools, though had to accept a "gentleman's agreement" with Japan to restrict future immigration. But he was a believer in the positive value of immigration and the contributions made by people who came to this country seeking to be Americans. In an oft-quoted message from 1919, dictated the day before he died, he laid down his views on the mutual responsibilities of the immigrant and his adopted country:

> *In the first place, we should insist that if the immigrant who comes here in good faith becomes an American and assimilates himself to us, he shall be treated on an exact equality with everyone else, for it is an outrage to discriminate against any such man because of creed, or birthplace, or origin. But this is predicated upon the person's becoming in every facet an American, and nothing but an American. . . . There can be no divided allegiance here. Any man who says he is an American, but something else also, isn't an American at all. We have room for but one flag, the American flag. . . . We have room for but one language here, and that is the English language. . . . And we have room for but one sole loyalty and that is a loyalty to the American people.*[14]

In 1915 Roosevelt denounced "hyphenated" Americans, those who held exclusionary allegiances to their places of origin, noting that "Americanism is a matter of the spirit and of the soul," and anyone "heartily and singly loyal to this Republic, then no matter where he was born, he is just as good an American as any one else." He warned that "the one absolutely certain way of bringing this nation to ruin, of preventing all possibility of its continuing to be a nation at all, would be to permit it to become a tangle of squabbling nationalities, an intricate knot of German-Americans, Irish-Americans, English-Americans, French-Americans, Scandinavian-Americans, or Italian-Americans, each preserving its separate nationality, each at heart feeling more sympathy with Europeans of that nationality than with the other citizens of the American Republic." In Roosevelt's view, the person who clings inordinately to cultural origins "plays a thoroughly mischievous part in the life of our body politic. He has no place here; and the sooner he returns to the land to which he feels his real heart-allegiance, the better it will be for every good American. There is no such thing as a hyphenated American who is a good American. The only man who is a good American is the man who is an American and nothing else."[15]

The 2008 Bradley Project Study found that most Americans still agree with Roosevelt's views. "The vast majority of Americans (89%) feel that Americanization or assimilation, through learning English and embracing American culture and values, is important to successful immigration, and most Americans (73%) believe that immigrants should be required to give up allegiance to their former nations upon becoming U.S. citizens."[16] Seventy-one percent backed making English the official language of the country, and only 1 percent felt that not knowing the language was unimportant. Those surveyed also believed that immigrants "should take an active role as citizens, and that a big part of that is immersing themselves in American culture and learning English." But younger people (ages 18–34) and "those who do not believe there is a unique national identity are much less likely to feel this way." [17] The 2011 Xavier study found that 54 percent agreed that "One of America's greatest strengths is that it has always been a beacon of opportunity to the rest of the world. People still yearn to come here for a better life," and 60 percent agreed that "immigration—people from all over the world coming to America for a better life—is important to keeping the American Dream alive."[18]

The Unwilling Americans

There are, of course, counter narratives to the immigrant experience. *The Uprooted,* Oscar Handlin's 1951 history, presented a view of peasants who came to the United States from Europe who were tossed out of their traditional lives and "cruelly carried to a distant land, and set to labor, unrewarding labor." In this view, immigration did not take place because people were coming here seeking to better themselves, they were thrust into circumstances beyond their control and did the best they could. For many if not most of them, their lives were poorer in America than in the old country, certainly poorer in spirit. The immigrants were not heroic pioneers but helpless victims.

African Americans have a compelling counter narrative because many of their ancestors were brought to America against their will. Once here they endured the institution of slavery, and there were significant restrictions even for those who managed to escape it. For example, the 1790 naturalization act explicitly applied only to "free whites." In the seminal 1857 Supreme Court case *Scott v. Sanford*, Associate Justice Peter Vivian Daniel wrote in a separate opinion that "the African race is not and never was recognised either by the language or purposes of the [Constitution], and it has been expressly excluded by every act of Congress providing for the creation of citizens by *naturalization*, these laws, as has already been remarked, being restricted to *free white aliens* exclusively." This argument was disposed of after the Civil War by the Thirteenth and Fourteenth Amendments, but subsequent state actions, particularly Jim Crow laws, made it difficult if not impossible for free blacks to enjoy the full benefits of citizenship. Institutionalized segregation, which was given the High Court's blessing in *Plessy v. Ferguson* (1896), further frustrated the ability of African Americans to assimilate into the broader culture. This system persisted until a century after the Civil War. So it is understandable that appeals to the ideals of the melting pot ring hollow in the black community. Nevertheless, 54 percent of Americans of African descent "feel that their traditions are quintessentially American." New immigrants from Africa, who have no familial connection to America's history of slavery, view their chosen country similarly to other immigrant groups.[19]

Native Americans as well have an understandably jaded view of the process. The history of the relationship between the Indians and the European migrants on both Western Hemisphere continents is long, bloody, and uninspiring. The U.S. reservation system is a relic of a perhaps beneficial recognition of the sovereign status of the Indian nations that predated the establishment of the United States.[20] But it also symbolizes the essential apartness and oppression that has characterized most relations between Indians and the government.

"Buenas días, mister"

Some Hispanic groups have also adopted the view that they are involuntary participants in the American experiment.[21] One Latino called his people "strangers in a native land. . . . Unlike previous immigrants most of us didn't come to America; instead, America came to us. Ours isn't just another immigrant's story, simply because assimilation may never be fully completed. . . . We may eat American food, buy American merchandise, and greet Americans daily with a 'Buenas días, mister' but at the core we will always remain untouched."[22] The notion that Hispanics—specifically Mexican Americans—are in the United States involuntarily is based on the belief that many if not most are descendants of Mexican nationals who lived in the area of the 1848 Mexican Cession. In their minds, this places them in the same category as African Americans or Indians as unwilling or conquered peoples, hence delegitimizing the United States and making failure to assimilate a form of indigenous resistance.

But most Mexican Americans have no blood ties to those who lived in the pre-1848 Mexican U.S. territories. There were only 13,000 Mexicans in the United States in 1850, and 11.9 million of the 12.7 million Mexicans in the United States in 2008 arrived after 1970.[23] The area of the cession was also barely Mexican in historical terms, having been part of that country during a scant 27-year window between 300 years of Spanish rule and becoming part of the United States. And those who want to assert some sort of validating indigenous tie would still have to explain why their claim to the land is more legitimate than those of the Hopi, Zuni, Navajo, Pueblo, and Apache tribes who had lived there when the Conquistadores showed up.[24]

The sense of separatism among some Hispanics does, to quote Theodore Roosevelt, play a thoroughly mischievous part in the life of our body politic. It has created numerous clashes over national rights and symbols, particularly in the Southwest. In May 2010, five students at Live Oak High School in Morgan Hill, California, were sent home for wearing clothing featuring the American flag.[25] Their offense: trespassing on Mexican heritage on Cinco de Mayo. Administrators called the flag-wearing "incendiary" and likely to cause violence. The school district overrode the decision, and the boys were allowed to return to school. In response, about two hundred students staged a walkout carrying Mexican flags.

The question is: Who taught these kids to hate America so much? There should be nothing disrespectful about the U.S. flag to Americans of Mexican descent or to any other immigrant group. Teaching children that their heritage is at odds with their citizenship promotes disunity and divisiveness. While the high school's administrators may have been responding to a real public-safety threat, that threat was the product of their failure to instill a sense of national pride in their students.

Incidents like this illustrate the poisonous effects that identity politics has on the nation. In the past, immigrant groups would attempt to outdo each other in demonstrating their patriotic attachment to the country that gave them safety, opportunity, and freedom. Today, immigrant activists think patriotism is at best an inconvenience, at worst a sellout. They have replaced the melting pot with hardening battle lines in a struggle for power.

The high school incident is only one example of Old Glory being forced into the closet. In 2006, a Colorado school seeking to placate Mexican nationalists banned the American flag. After a mass student protest, Mexican flags were banned as well. In 2008,

Dos Palos, California, high school student Jake Shelly was forced to remove a red, white, and blue tie-dyed American-flag T-shirt he had worn to school because he was in violation of a dress code banning "shirts/blouses that promote specific races, cultures, or ethnicities." In 2007, students at Hobbton High School in Sampson County, North Carolina, were not allowed to wear American-flag-themed clothes on the anniversary of the September 11, 2001, attacks because of a general school prohibition on garments featuring flags. The superintendent of schools said that "educators didn't want to be forced to pick and choose which flags should be permissible."

However not all flags are created equal. Some flags may be fashion statements, but the American flag is the patriotic symbol of the nation in which we live. This is why the American flag flies outside American schools as opposed to, say, Zimbabwe's. The Stars and Stripes should be a proud statement of unity for all, but sadly this is not always the case. Schools should spend less time telling patriotic students not to cause a ruckus simply by wearing the national colors and more time teaching the kids who are offended by the American flag how wrongheaded their views are. This might require teachers and administrators to begin making value judgments and moral choices for the benefit of the children they are charged with educating, but that should be their job.

"The notion of endless opportunity for all in the American Dream," one critic observed, "is routinely invoked by those who are unconcerned about the inherent inequality in capitalism or ignore the deeply embedded white supremacy that expresses itself in institutional and unconscious racism, which constrains indigenous, black, and Latino people in the United States."[26] But according to a recent survey these "oppressed" peoples are actually the most hopeful about achieving success in America. The March 2011 study by Xavier University's Center for the Study of the American Dream found that on a scale of 1 to 10, where 10 means the best possible condition of the dream and 1 means the worst possible condition,

Latinos gave the dream the highest rating of any demographic group, with 47 percent rating it between 6 and 10. The second highest ratings came from immigrants, and third were "people of color."[27]

The study found that, in general, first- and second-generation immigrants, regardless of their country of origin, were much more optimistic than the general population. Forty percent felt the country is headed in the right direction, compared to 23 percent of the country at large. Forty-eight percent rate the dream in good condition, compared to 31 percent of the population overall. And while 39 percent of all the population believes America still represents the future, this view was held by 48 percent of immigrants.[28] Studies like this show that despite high-profile incidents of America bashing and media campaigns from pressure groups, the fundamental spirit of the immigrants is the same as it was when Emma Lazarus penned the immortal words at the base of the Statue of Liberty.

American Muslims

Muslim Americans have recently taken center stage as an immigrant group purportedly facing a difficult transition. Pressure groups, commentators, and politicians have promoted the idea of a rising tide of post-9/11 Islamophobia. This narrative is guided by the victimology model, but there is no empirical backing for it. The latest FBI annual crime statistics report showed that 13.2 percent of religiously based attacks (160 incidents) were directed at Muslims, compared to 65.4 percent (887 incidents) directed at Jews.[29] There were also more incidents of antiblack, antiwhite, anti-Hispanic, and antihomosexual hate crimes than anti-Muslim crimes. And of 149 deaths by hate-crime over fifteen years (1996–2010), not one victim was a Muslim. This does not mean that Muslims have nothing to worry about or do not need to defend their image, but it does suggest that the ongoing media frenzy over alleged American

Islamophobia is overblown. Nevertheless, President Obama has made it a personal crusade to defend Muslims against this nonexistent threat, and thereby promotes the notion that Americans are as intolerant as the multiculturalists say they are.[30]

At a White House interfaith dinner honoring Ramadan in September 2009, the president noted that Muslim American women can wear the hijab but managed to demean the country in the process. He recognized Nashala Hearn, who was present at the dinner, whose school mistakenly forbade her from wearing a hijab under a dress code that banned bandanas and other head coverings, including hats. The policy was altered later, but the president omitted the salient details and made it sound as though the school was actively practicing religious discrimination. The foreign dignitaries present at the dinner might have benefited more from hearing that thousands of women freely wear the hijab in this country without a problem and, more important, that Muslim women in America also are free not to cover their heads if they choose. Instead, Mr. Obama tried to fabricate a Rosa Parks moment with the takeaway that America discriminates, when it does not.

Mr. Obama said, "The contribution of Muslims to the United States are too long to catalog because Muslims are so interwoven into the fabric of our communities and our country." But this can hardly be true; Muslims are a small minority in the country, and 63 percent of them are foreign born. It is no slight to acknowledge that most Muslims are relative newcomers to the United States and lack the numbers and longevity to have made as significant a contribution to the country as other groups. Instead of saying "the best is yet to come"—which would be a reasonable statement showing hope for the future—the president chose to engage in the worst sort of identity-politics pandering, inventing a history and tradition where none exists. In his 2010 Ramadan message, Mr. Obama upped the ante, claiming that "Islam has always been part of America."[31] Yet Islam had no influence on the origins and development of the United States, contributed nothing to early American political culture, art, literature, music, or any other aspect of the early nation. No other group would expect to be credited with invented contributions to American history. Hindus are not diminished because they were not represented at Valley Forge. Greek Orthodox Americans would not expect to be written into the first Thanksgiving. Mr. Obama does no favors to Muslims by giving Islam a prominence in American annals that it has not yet earned.

The White House approach is predictably true to the tenets of multiculturalism, but it is bad for the country, and for Muslims. Instead of fabricating a climate of hate to portray Muslims as overcoming significant obstacles to live freely in the United States, or inventing an American Muslim history that does not exist, it is better to see Muslims as one of the latest groups to contribute to the melting pot, at least for those willing to assimilate.

A 2011 study by the Pew Research Center found that most American Muslims are much like any other Americans. "Muslim Americans look similar to the rest of the public," the report said. "Comparable percentages say they watch entertainment television, follow professional or college sports, recycle household materials, and play video games."[32] Fifty-six percent were satisfied with the way things were going in the country, compared to 23 percent of the public at large. Seventy-four percent agreed that most people can get ahead if they are willing to work hard, compared to 62 percent among the general public. And they did not buy in to the victimology mindset; only 16 percent believed the general public is unfriendly toward Muslim Americans, and the figure drops to 7 percent among immigrants who have arrived in the last twenty years.

Even more compelling are the data that relate to the workings of the melting pot. Thirteen percent of Muslims have married outside their faith (compared to 8 percent of Christians). Fifty one percent reported that few to none of their close friends were Muslims. Less than half attend services weekly or pray five times a day and, according to a Pew religious commitment index, only 29 percent are highly religious, while 22 percent are barely observant, if at all. The last is the more important statistic. Muslims in general do not come to the United States because they are fleeing religious persecution. If anything, the freedom they enjoy here that they did not have in their native lands is the freedom to be less religious.[33]

"If you live in this country, you have to live like an American," said Mohammed Mohammed, a resident of Alexandria, Louisiana. The native of Jordan and Louisiana Tech alum came to the United States in 1985 and made a life for himself, owning and operating four convenience stores and raising six children. He found that the ways of the old country were hard to hang onto. "A few years ago I tried to take my family overseas, and we had a difficult time," he said. "The customs are different. I realized, then, that I was also different." He believed that his children would not "carry on traditions and customs that they have not been exposed to" and that this represented "the end of our culture. The next generation will be 100 percent American."[34]

In some cities one can witness a very American scene of a multigenerational family from the Middle East out for a walk. The older generation is wearing the garb of their home country, maybe speaking their native language; the middle generation is looking very middle class and put together; and the kids are dressed like every other American kid, with clothes from the Gap or Target, plugged into some kind of electronic device, and exuding that sense of easy confidence that comes naturally to young people who grow up in the American culture. The United States is a country where Muslims have the freedom to worship in the manner they choose. But it is also a country where, unlike in most of their homelands, they are free to eat pork, marry a Buddhist, and ignore the call to prayer. This is the more important freedom—the freedom to choose, the freedom that for four centuries has brought immigrants to America.

nine

THE NATIVE AMERICANS

Everyone in the United States comes from somewhere, has some roots, some attachment to the ore placed in the melting pot. A person may be close to the source or not—first generation, second, third, maybe unknown. Perhaps the family tree has recent arrivals on one side and a long American history on the other. There are limitless combinations in the country, the result of the generative and fruitful mixture of peoples, the product of love and family and heritage.

Ancestry can be very meaningful to a person or a family, or it can mean little. It could be an identifier based on a surname or close contact with relatives from the "old county." It can be a connection to a place where a person grew up, an ethnic neighborhood, an enclave. One's ancestral culture could be transmitted through surroundings or passed down through families. The tie can be strong, but it can also be weak, or even nonexistent. For every American who idealizes his or her roots, there are even greater numbers for whom their ancestors' national origins convey little meaning, if any. An Irish surname might be significant to a person only on St. Patrick's Day, and even then be interpreted in an American cultural context, which tends to involve drinking at a pub with a neon shamrock in the window. Maybe the bartender is an Irish immigrant, or perhaps someone from Barbados. The same is true of other nationalities. As Karl Cole of the Federation of German-American Societies of Buffalo [New York] and Vicinity noted that "a lot of people don't come to German festivals to hear the old-time ballads and music. They just come for the parties afterward. In the next twenty years or so, people won't even know where their roots started."[1]

An ethnic identity could just be a form of personal branding—lacking strong family traditions, one may latch onto the identity from a country one has never visited and knows nothing about. And in a meaningful sense the countries that one's ancestors left fifty or a hundred or more years ago no longer exist. People may point with justifiable pride to ancestors who came over from Ireland in the mid-nineteenth century and made a life in America. But these descendants are American, not Irish, and the Ireland of the time of the Great Famine from which their ancestors departed is long gone. People may have relatives who came from German kingdoms that have vanished along with their ways of life, or from Tsarist-era shtetls in Russia that pogroms, Soviet collectivization, the Second World War, and the Holocaust rendered extinct. China and Japan have changed drastically from the time of the "Yellow Peril." Or maybe someone is a recent immigrant from West Africa who escaped from a village wracked by ethnic conflict, came to America, and never looked back. "Even though we may have Celtic crosses hanging up or African art on the wall or things we identify with our heritage, we have a lot more in common as Americans," said Dennis Connors of the Onondaga [New York] Historical Association. "An African American and an Irish American probably have a lot more in common [with each other] than an Irish American has in common with an Irish person over in Ireland."[2]

Memories are preserved in family histories, in communities, and in countless traditions and observances. But collective memories fade as people age and pass away, and traditions become diluted as families disperse and merge with other families. Through this winnowing the best of the old persists and the rest falls away, leaving an idealized vision and sense of pride in one's roots. For most multigenerational Americans, this evolution can involve links to a number of countries of origin and whole branches of the family tree that have faded in the mists of time and memory.

Ethnicity and the Census

Ancestry, ethnicity, and race are complex issues for individuals, but the government prefers to keep it simple. The census, the American Community Survey, and countless government forms force people to reduce their rich history and personal identity to a series of preset responses. The government does not classify people to cater to the academic interests of demographers, but collects data "to enforce provisions under the Civil Rights Act which prohibit discrimination based upon race, sex, religion, and national origin." The data on ancestry or ethnic origin are used to "measure the social and economic characteristics of ethnic groups and to tailor services to accommodate cultural differences."[3]

The census has long asked questions about race, going back to 1790. The race question is a matter of some controversy since it requires the government to establish categories, and for people voluntarily—though under threat of punishment—to place themselves into one of them. This is the multiculturalist dream, a box for every person and every person in a box. But not everyone likes being reduced to a racial profile. It is impossible to achieve a colorblind society when the state requires people to define themselves in ways that divide them. It is the reverse of the ideal of the melting pot, and the more data the government collects, the more room there is for bureaucratic mischief.

The government imposes and continually reinforces awareness of differences; it mandates official racial and ethnic identities, and bestows special benefits, at least on some. "To be without a race-ethnic group identity in the United States today is to be without an identity," one study concluded. "In many contexts—from schools and universities to employment to health care to housing—often several times a year, one must be able to tell a race-ethnic group identity story: 'I am a _____-American.'"[4] The old self-interest in assimilation and Americanism has been replaced with a new self-interest that emphasizes and rewards differences. In this sense, the American who rejects the hyphen is not a good citizen but one who is practicing unilateral disarmament.

Some see the emphasis on race and ancestry as an assault on the American ideal of equality. "Fully one-quarter of the space on this year's [2010] form is taken up with questions of race and ethnicity," Mark Krikorian wrote in *National Review Online*, "which are clearly illegitimate and none of the government's business." He recommended building a "needed wall of separation between race and state." He proposed that rather than self-identifying one of the listed races people instead check the box marked "Some other race" and write in American. "It's a truthful answer," he wrote, "but at the same time is a way for ordinary citizens to express their rejection of unconstitutional racial classification schemes. . . . So remember: Question 9—'Some other race'—'American.' Pass it on."[5]

Self-describing as an "American" can be more than just an act of civil disobedience, nonviolent resistance, or individual protest against a system of racial classification. It is not just a rejection of other ethnic or national roots, but a specific statement, a claim on a culture, a history, and an idea. Asserting an American identity means to step out of the established official framework and launch into the terra icognita of the ideal citizen. The Americans have cut themselves free from other cultures, free from government categories, and stand on their own, sui generis.

Who Are the Americans?

"American" is not accepted as an official racial classification, but has established itself as a valid category of U.S. ancestry. The census first began asking about ancestry in 1980, on the long form mailed to one in six American households. The top five responses were English (50 million), German (49 million), Irish (40 million), African American (21 million), and French (13 million). Not included on this list were the 13.3 million respondents (5.9% of the country) who wrote in "American." Had it been reported with the other data it would have been the fifth largest ancestry group, edging out French. But because "American" did not fit the research model, it was considered a mistake and coded as "ancestry not specified." A later report explained that "respondents were instructed to provide a response which referred to their nationality group, lineage or country in which they or their ancestors were born before their arrival in the United States," and that "a single response of 'American' or 'United States'" was not deemed responsive to the question.[6] "The consensus was, it wasn't a real ancestry," said Angela Bingham, a Census Bureau demographer.[7] "It's clear from the question that they are looking for people to not give 'American' as an answer," said Professor Christine Himes of Syracuse University. "To choose 'American' you have to be a rebel in a way."[8] But that was precisely the point.

The number of Americans was too large to ignore, and in the 1990 census it was "accepted as a unique ethnicity if it was given alone, with an ambiguous response (such as 'mixed' or 'adopted'), or with state names."[9] The overall ancestry numbers shifted—German was first with 58 million, followed by Irish (39 million), English (33 million), African American (24 million), and Italian (15 million). The large shifts in numbers of some of the major ancestry groups no doubt reflected the methodological problems in asking citizens to pinpoint a specific single major ancestry when many are of mixed heritage, not to mention the subjectivity inherent in the question. There is also the power of suggestion; in 1990 "German" was listed as one of the examples in the question, which might explain its jump to the top of the list. Croatian ancestry, the other example that year, more than doubled.[10] Thirteen million reported as solely American, and the report noted that the "percent of persons reporting 'American' ancestry was very similar between 1980 and 1990 (5.9 and 5.2 percent, respectively). . . . The regions experienced a decline in the percent reporting 'American' with the exception of the South, which had a slightly higher percentage reporting 'American.'"[11]

In the 2000 census the top five ancestry groups were German (15.2%), Irish (10.8%), African American (8.8%), English (8.7%) and American (7.2%). Over twenty million people declared American as their sole ancestry, and the jump from 1990 was the "largest numerical growth of any group in the 1990s," a 58 percent increase.[12] "People may have reported American as their ancestry for several reasons," the Census Bureau reported, "including multiple ethnic backgrounds, an unknown ethnic background, national pride, citizenship status, or ancestors that have been here for a long time."[13] Another trend in the 2000 census was a rise in the number of people who left the ancestry item blank, which can be interpreted as either not knowing or a form of protest.[14]

After 2000 the census shifted the ancestry question from the long form of the decennial census to the ongoing American Community Survey (ACS). The number of Americans reported by the ACS has shifted over the years, staying around twenty million and ranging roughly from 7 to 9 percent. Methodology continues to be an issue in finding an accurate count; even in the 2000 census when people mentioned American plus another ancestry the other was counted as the sole response. A drop in the proportion of Americans between two surveys "may have been caused by methodological differences," according to a 2008 Census Bureau report. "American is an acceptable and widely used ancestry. . . . Some researchers, however, may be interested in more specific ethnic background information, and may prefer to see fewer responses of American and a higher proportion of responses that reflect specific countries or ethnic groups."[15] The ACS also inexplicably treats African ancestry as an "other" category, which makes interpreting those data more difficult.

The United States of Americans

Americans are found all over the country. The states with the most Americans are, in descending order, Texas, Florida, North Carolina, Georgia, Ohio, Kentucky, and California. Americans are in the top five ancestry groups, by percentage, in twenty-seven states stretching from Maine to Washington, and the plurality in Kentucky, West Virginia, Tennessee, and Arkansas.

Some counties with large numbers of Americans include: Maricopa County, Arizona; Los Angeles, Orange, and San Diego Counties in California; Broward, Hillsborough, Lee, Miami-Dade, and Orange Counties in Florida; Dallas and Harris Counties in Texas; Cook County, Illinois; Wake County, North Carolina; and Kings County, New York. Americans are the plurality in a mostly contiguous group of counties in the southeast United States, in an area west of the 1763 "proclamation line," the first parts of America that were claimed by the colonies as their own in defiance of royal authority. It overlaps Appalachia, though is not limited to that area. These core American counties stretch from the eastern Appalachian foothills in a cone west, roughly south of the Ohio River, across southern Missouri and Arkansas and into east Texas. Above-average percentages of Americans are found in all of the states surrounding this core group, from Ohio to Florida and Texas to the Carolinas. Counties with greater than 20 percent Americans are in Kentucky, Tennessee, West Virginia, western Virginia, northern Alabama, and southern Georgia, and scattered in the surrounding states. The epicenter is in southeastern Kentucky, the oldest settled area outside the original thirteen colonies, which has been bypassed by many subsequent waves of immigration; in southeastern Kentucky the proportions of Americans can range up to 50 percent.

The counties with plurality concentrations of Americans correspond to the area tagged "Dixie" in Joel Garreau's 1984 book, *Nine Nations of North America*. But to the extent that nickname carries overtones of the Confederacy, it is important to note that the areas with the highest concentrations of Americans are also the parts of the South where slavery and the plantation culture did not have a foothold. Rather, these were the areas of the South with the most pro-Union sentiment, most dramatically in West Virginia, the only state that was carved out of another state, specifically because the people there had voted against leaving the Union in the May 23, 1861, Virginia secession referendum.

The area with the highest concentrations of Americans mirrors that described by cultural historian Colin Woodard as Greater Appalachia. This area was "founded in the early eighteenth century by wave upon wave of rough, bellicose settlers from the war-ravaged borderlands of northern Ireland, northern England, and the Scottish lowlands." They transplanted a culture formed in a state of near-constant warfare and upheaval, characterized by "a warrior ethic and a deep commitment to personal sovereignty and individual liberty." Over the centuries the people there have been "intensely suspicious of lowland aristocrats and Yankee social engineers alike," and have "shifted alliances based on whoever appeared to be the greatest threat to their freedom." Their main objective in contemporary times is to "undo the federal government's ability to overrule local preferences." Woodard points out that the area "has had a near monopoly on the production of 'southern' populists (LBJ, Ross Perot, Sam Rayburn, Mike Huckabee) and progressives (Cordell Hull, Bill Clinton, Al Gore)."[16] Others of note from this area include Presidents Andrew Jackson, James K. Polk, Zachary Taylor, Abraham Lincoln, Andrew Johnson, Ulysses S. Grant, and Harry Truman.

The "Bitter Clingers"

Looking at the areas with high concentrations of Americans conjures various impressions: The Bible Belt. Rednecks. Flyover country. Hillbillies. NASCAR country. WalMart. Waffle House. Cracker Barrel. Country music. The area below the sweet tea line, or in the "Coke" zone. The stereotypic view would be of a white, rural, lower-middle-class (if not below), less-educated population. This was summed up in April 2008, when then-Senator Obama told the audience at a San Francisco fundraiser about his experiences campaigning in small-town America:

> *You go into some of these small towns in Pennsylvania, a lot like a lot of small towns in the Midwest, the jobs have been gone now for twenty-five years and nothing's replaced them. And they fell through the Clinton administration, and the Bush administration, and each successive administration has said that somehow these communities are gonna regenerate, and they have not. So it's not surprising then that they get bitter, they cling to guns or religion or antipathy towards people who aren't like them or anti-immigrant sentiment or anti-trade sentiment as a way to explain their frustrations.*[17]

Mr. Obama later admitted that his characterization was "bone-headed," and of course when politicians are caught saying things like that out loud it always is. But it no doubt resonated with his wealthy, elite, liberal San Francisco audience. They probably shared his stereotyped view of the "bitter clingers," the denizens of flyover country. He could have thrown in references to tin shacks, moonshine, snake handling, and banjo picking, and his audience would not have blinked, because it fits the contemporary urban left-wing cosmopolitan view of the "unfortunates" who are "stuck" in that part of the country. Their perspective on the area and its people is something akin to the "before" scenes in a Tennessee Valley Authority propaganda film, or any part of the movie *Deliverance*.

Shortly after Mr. Obama's "bitter clinger" statement, Nate Silver identified American ancestry in his "FiveThirtyEight" political blog as a key variable in predicting areas that would favor Hillary Clinton in the 2008 Democratic primaries. "To be perfectly blunt," he wrote, "this variable seems to serve as a pretty good proxy for folks that a lot of us elitists would usually describe as 'rednecks.' And for whatever reason, these 'American' voters do not like Barack Obama. That is why he's getting killed in the polls in Kentucky and West Virginia, for instance, where there are high concentrations of them."[18] This turned out to be a good prediction. In the 2008 general election, while most areas of the country showed large or small shifts toward the Democratic candidate compared to the 2004 election (as one would expect), the core areas of American ethnicity more or less moved in the opposite direction.

But the assumption that those identifying as American are mainly lower-middle-class back-country hicks is wrong. According to the 2010 ACS survey, 12 million of the 20 million Americans live in urban centers, and only eight million live in rural areas.[19] Thus, although proportionately more Americans are rural, the majority live in or around cities. For example, maps included in the 2000 census report show Atlanta and Dallas-Ft. Worth surrounded by American pluralities.

Areas with high populations of Americans are not monochromatic. For example, more than fifteen thousand people live in

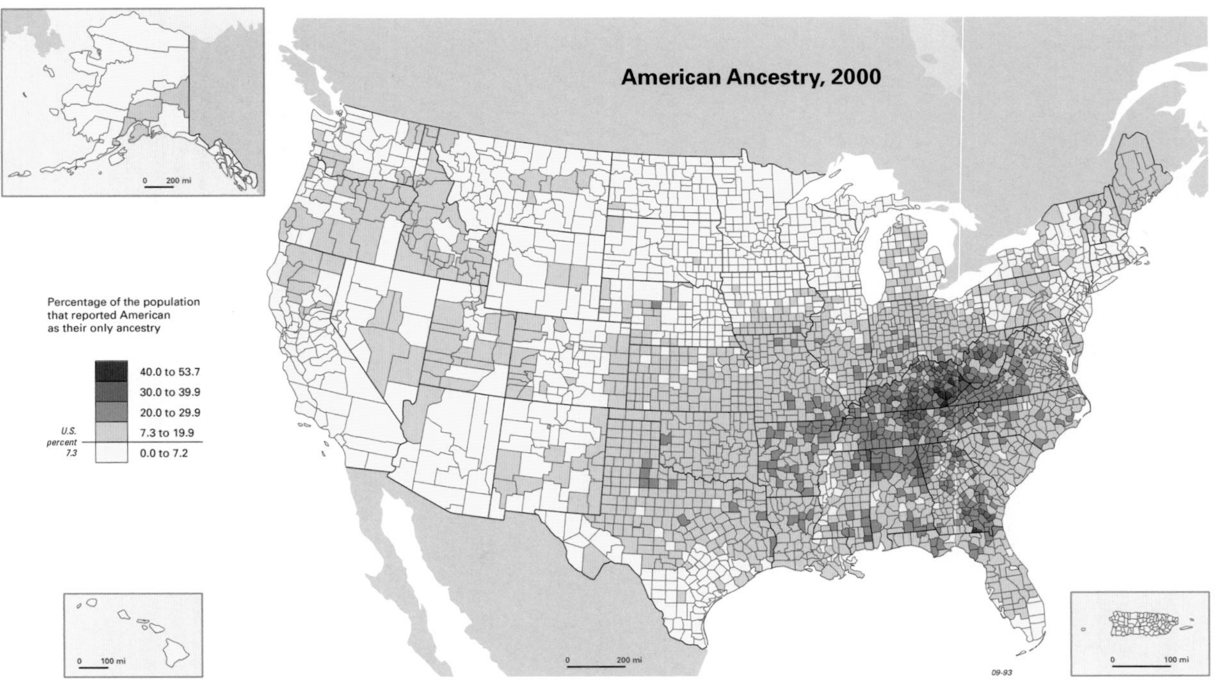

Americans are found all over the country. The states with the most Americans are Texas, Florida, North Carolina, Georgia, Ohio, Kentucky, and California. Source: U.S. Census Bureau. "Ancestry." *Census Atlas of the United States*. Series CENSR-29. Washington, DC, 2007: p. 142. http://www.census.gov/population/www/cen2000/censusatlas/. Created by International Mapping for the U.S. Census Bureau.

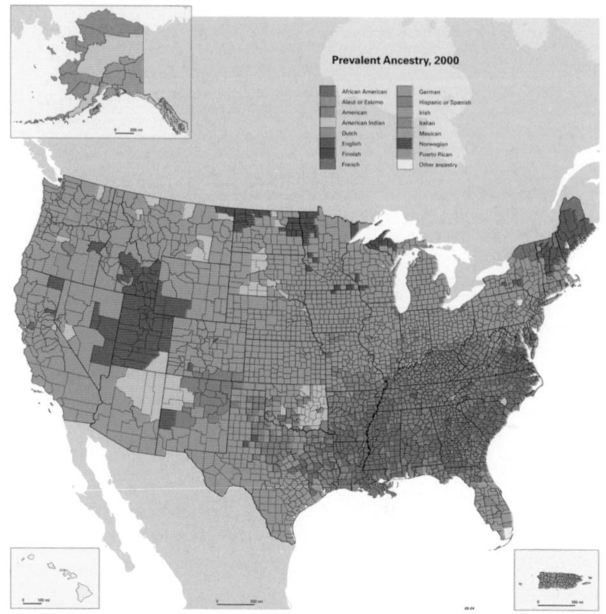

The core American counties stretch from the eastern Appalachian foothills in a cone west, roughly south of the Ohio River, across southern Missouri and Arkansas and into east Texas. Source: U.S. Census Bureau. "Ancestry." *Census Atlas of the United States*. Series CENSR-29. Washington, DC, 2007: p. 141. http://www.census.gov/population/www/cen2000/censusatlas/. Created by International Mapping for the U.S. Census Bureau.

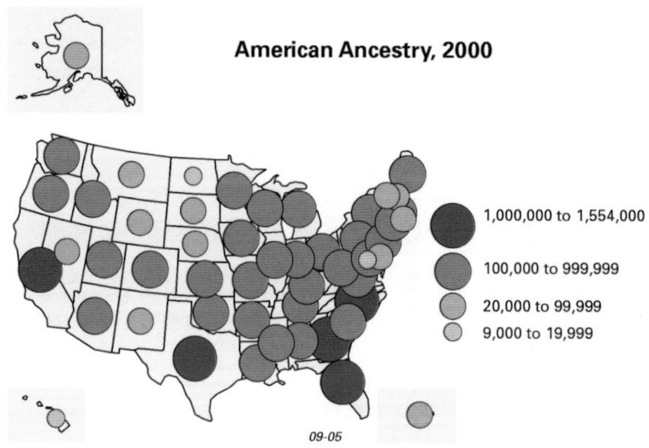

The epicenter of Americans is in southeastern Kentucky. Proportions of Americans can range up to 50 percent. Source: U.S. Census Bureau. "Ancestry." *Census Atlas of the United States*. Series CENSR-29. Washington, DC, 2007: p. 155. http://www.census.gov/population/www/cen2000/censusatlas/. Created by International Mapping for the U.S. Census Bureau.

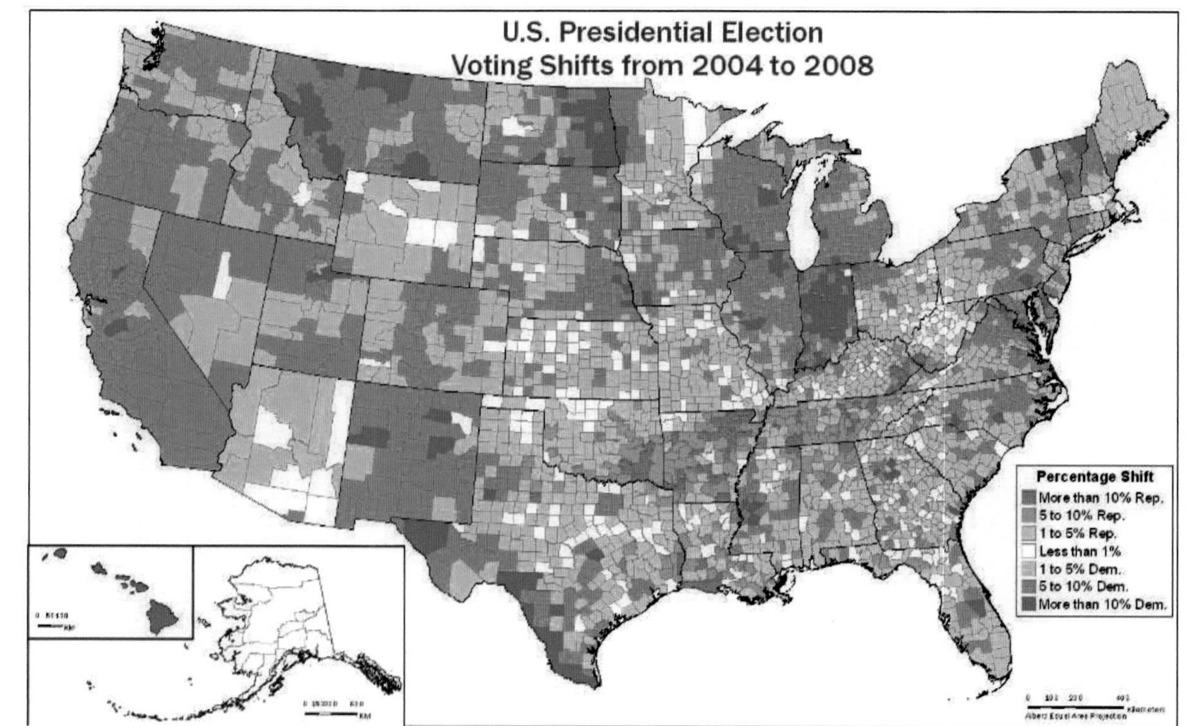

In the 2008 general election, while most areas of the country showed shifts towards the Democratic candidate compared to the 2004 election, the core areas of American ethnicity moved more or less in the opposite direction. Source: Karl Musser. Wikimedia Commons. 19 February 2009, http://en.wikipedia.org/wiki/File:US_Election04-08shift.png.

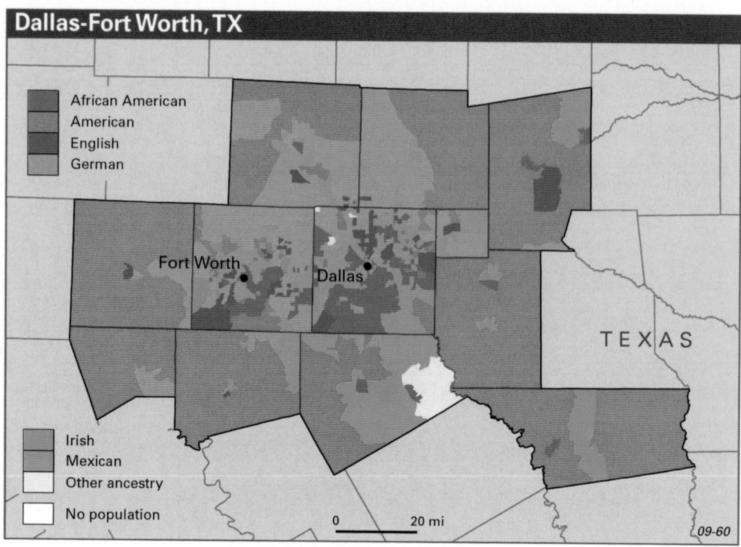

While proportionately Americans are more rural, the majority live in or around cities. Source: U.S. Census Bureau. "Ancestry." *Census Atlas of the United States.* Series CENSR-29. Washington, DC, 2007: p. 147. http://www.census.gov/population/www/cen2000/censusatlas/. Created by International Mapping for the U.S. Census Bureau.

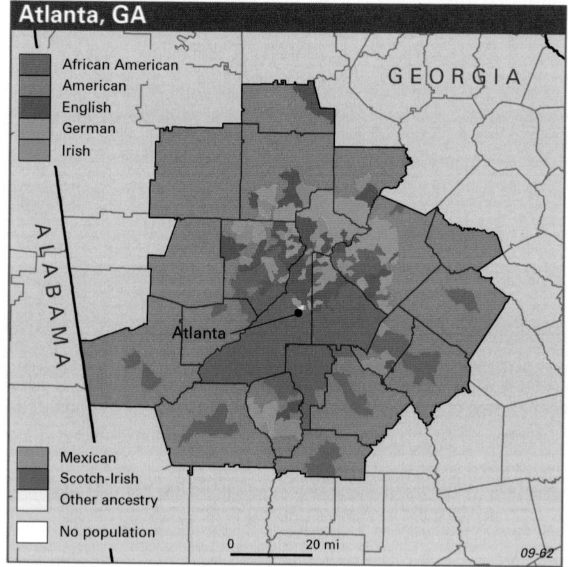

While proportionately Americans are more rural, the majority live in or around cities. Source: U.S. Census Bureau. "Ancestry." *Census Atlas of the United States.* Series CENSR-29. Washington, DC, 2007: p. 147. http://www.census.gov/population/www/cen2000/censusatlas/. Created by International Mapping for the U.S. Census Bureau.

zip code 40965, near Middlesboro, Kentucky, along the border with Tennessee and Virginia. Of them, almost half are Americans, and the other major ethnic groups self-identify as being of Greek, African, Egyptian, English, Irish, or Lebanese ancestry.

In other respects, Americans are demographically almost identical to the rest of the country. Fifty-one percent of Americans are women. The average family size is three. Americans are slightly younger than the rest of the country. Their household income is 90 percent of the national mean, but there are fewer Americans below the poverty line. They have a somewhat lower proportion of four-year college graduates (16%, versus 24% nationally) but have slightly higher percentages of home ownership and military service.

Their jobs are typical: 30 percent are in management, business, science, and arts occupations; 27 percent in sales; 16 percent in service jobs; 14 percent in production, transportation, and material moving; and 11 percent in natural resources, construction, and maintenance. Like most people in the United States, they work mainly in the health care, retail, manufacturing, and construction industries, and only 2.4 percent are involved in agriculture, forestry, fishing and hunting, and mining. The most significant differences are predictable—only .17 percent is foreign born, against 11.05 percent nationally, and 3 percent speak a language other than English at home, against 18 percent in the United States as a whole.[20]

American: It's What We Are

Staking the claim to American ethnicity is a conscious break with history, race, or any other ties. It reflects a state of mind, a self-awareness. Warren Brown, a Cornell University demographer, said, "you're probing people's active consciousness and what they claim and say rather than some scientific genealogical probe."[21] The millions of people staking their claim to American ancestry are rising above the divisions in the country and also accepting the fundamental diversity of the United States. "We are not threatened by ethnic backgrounds now," said Michael Marsden, provost at Eastern Kentucky University. "We are at peace with the American cultural frame. People realized for the first time that real strength comes in American diversity. I think we realized that we can be different but, at the same time, the same."[22] Lewis Carlson, retired director of the Western Michigan American Studies Program, said, "People who call themselves American simply do so because they realize [Americans] are not one ethnic group and people are comfortable with that."[23]

For others, being an American is taking a personal stand. Lawrence Bowden of Randolph-Macon Women's College said, "Being an American is the attitude one takes toward oneself. The people who say they are American are tapping into a notion that Americans have always loved their country and are proud of where they are, and more importantly, who they are. It is embedded in everything we do and value."[24] Seventy-four-year-old Gerald Fuller Sr. of Craig County, Virginia, summed up "American" as "loyalty to the country, freedom, the right to make choices and the right to bear arms."[25] Thomas Marlin Landis of the small town of Mexico, Pennsylvania, said that people wrote American on the census because, "well, that's what we are."[26]

Many people would agree. If asked directly, most people in the United States claim to be American.[27] A 2001 survey showed that 83 percent of the country's residents "identify their culture and traditions as uniquely 'American.'" This is particularly true of those of European heritage, but "a majority of residents of Latin American descent (61 percent), African descent (54 percent), and Middle Eastern descent (64 percent) also feel that their traditions are quintessentially American."[28]

The Bradley Project found that 84 percent of people in the U.S. believe there is "a unique American national identity based on shared beliefs, values, and culture." The most important defining characteristic of the identity, according to the survey, is freedom. Yet 63 percent feel that the identity is growing weaker, and a quarter of Americans believe that "since there are so many different ethnic groups and cultures in the U.S., there is no single definition of what it means to be an American." This feeling is strongest among younger people, which points to a future of a less-shared sense of identity.[29]

To the extent there is a shared identity in the country, it is a choice to recognize it and not cling to divisions that should mean little in an American context. Families and peoples that have been in this country for one, or two, or four centuries should not consider themselves to be from someplace else. Many countries have arisen in the last four hundred years, and many ethnicities have built their national myths in a shorter time than the United States has existed. Americans think of themselves as a young people, but the Zulu nation of South Africa with all its traditions and royal lineage was a minor and unimportant tribe until the late eighteenth century. The House of Saud emerged as a force around the same time, and only became Saudi Arabia in the twentieth century. Latin Americans in their various nationalities are all products of migrations, conquests, and intermarriages taking place since the New World was discovered. This is also true of Caribbean peoples, many originally brought in servitude but now not only free and self-ruling but also with distinct and unique cultures.

The four hundred years from Jamestown and Plymouth is long enough to have formed a distinct culture and people. And while the American melting pot has been continually renewed, refreshed, and made vibrant with the mixture of new peoples, they come to live under one of the oldest continuing governments and written constitutions in the world. If people can be said to be rooted in shared language, foundational stories, history, experience, culture, belief systems, national myths, and political culture—all the things that make a people outside of blood and land—then the Americans are a people.

ten

THE AMERICAN FUTURE

Poet and author Richard Brautigan was a counterculture icon of the 1960s. He was a favorite of hippies and other free spirits, and his writings were staples in college English departments. Yet beneath the long hair and wire-rimmed glasses ran a deep, almost primordial strain of Americanism. The actor Dennis Hopper, a friend of his, told the story of a night when they were both drinking and how "[Brautigan] said he was very much against any kind of social welfare. He felt that if people couldn't help themselves the government shouldn't help them, and he kept saying that America would only be remembered for maybe another hundred years and then the idea would be a dream, a word people would repeat like a fantasy, as if it all had been an idealized moment in the past."[1] Forty years later the idea of America as an idealized moment destined to fade does not seem so far-fetched.

The Idea of American Decline

In his 2012 State of the Union speech, President Obama said, "Anyone who tells you that America is in decline or that our influence has waned doesn't know what they're talking about." But the statement was belied by the fact that he felt it necessary to make it. In foreign and domestic affairs there is a palpable and growing sense that the United States can no longer influence events to the extent that it once could. The Obama administration has attempted to make a virtue of this weakness, for example by promoting the notion of "leading from behind." However, liberal intellectuals seem torn between trying to deny that the decline is taking place and embracing it as a long overdue check on U.S. arrogance.

Most attention in the debate over the decline is paid to waning U.S. influence abroad. The heady days immediately after the collapse of communism are long gone. There is little talk of the United States as the world's sole remaining superpower, of the global hegemon, or of Fukuyama's "end of history." Mr. Obama said that "America remains the one indispensable nation in world affairs," but events during his administration have conspired to demonstrate otherwise.[2] There is a growing sense internationally that the world will keep turning without the United States.

This is not the first time that America has been said to be in decline. A European observer wrote of "the long, uninterrupted, deplorable decline of America from a moderately conservative federal republic to the despotism of an ignorant, centralized democracy"—this in 1876.[3] Another commentator bemoaned the fact that the United States "produces fewer inventors than of old" and blamed the influx of foreign workers and centralization of big business for the "apparent decline of America's inventive powers"—in 1907.[4] Talk of decline was widespread seventy years later, when the Watergate scandal, defeat in Vietnam, and the "malaise" of the Carter years sapped American confidence.[5] Even during the robust Reagan era, opponents of his policies predicted ultimate doom. Paul Kennedy's *The Rise and Fall of Great Powers,* first published in 1987, sought to give historical backing to the then-current critique that increased military spending would break the American economy and lead to its ultimate decline. The best that could be done, Kennedy concluded, was to manage the coming crash.[6] Of course, when the crash came, it was on the other side of the Iron Curtain. Contemporary echoes of the argument that wars have drained the government's coffers must contend with the fact that ten years of war in Afghanistan cost far less than the Obama administration's one-shot 2009 economic "stimulus" program.[7]

Robert Kagan, in *The World America Made*, published in 2012, argues that talk of U.S. decline is a straw man.[8] Many declinists vastly overestimate past American power and thus set a false standard against which to judge the present. The argument has merit; much of America's relative power in the years after the Second World War were the result of the war itself: economies were destroyed, empires were falling, and Soviet communism was on the march. The United States was relatively untouched by the war's destructive effects, hence was the last country standing. Those who raise the alarm about the declining U.S. share of the world's gross domestic product are talking about a trend that began in 1951. The real boom times for America, when relatively robust economic growth reaped greater and greater shares of world GDP, were between the end of the Civil War in 1865 and the onset of the Great Depression. In those days the British were the ones debating whether their empire was or would ever be in decline, and American expatriate author Henry James mused on "the Americans looming up—dim, vast, portentous—in their millions like gathering waves—the barbarians of the Roman Empire."[9]

Breaking the Social Contract

But the analogy to Rome is not best expressed by "barbarians at the gates." Receding U.S. military and economic influence abroad are symptoms of decline that do not speak to the cause. While analysts are looking at the margins, the rot has come from within.

The potentially fatal decline is not in the power of the United States but in the idea of America. The Rome analogy should not look to the barbarian invasions of the late Empire, but to the end of the Republic in the time of Cicero.

Public regard for the American political system is at low ebb. In the annual Gallup poll asking about public trust in American institutions, those that speak to local concerns or civic pride always top the list: the military, small business, the police, and organized religion. At the bottom are institutions that connote remoteness, perceived corruption, or lack of concern about the people: the press, banks, big business and labor, HMOs, and—lately at the bottom of the list—the United States Congress. In the June 2011 poll, only 12 percent of Americans expressed a great deal or quite a lot of confidence in the Congress. This contrasts with 88 percent expressing confidence in the military. Members of both political parties give Congress a positive rating in the low teens, and approval from independents is a mere 7 percent.[10] The 2011 Xavier study showed similar results, with politics in general, big business, government, and the media topping the list of institutions losing trust, and the military and religious organizations gaining trust.[11] The Bradley Project found that when asked which groups shared their values, enlisted soldiers (70%) and K–12 teachers (65%) were at the top of the list, and members of the news media (31%) and U.S. political leaders (29%) were at the bottom.[12] An April 2012 Pew Center poll showed that solid majorities had favorable views of state and local governments, while faith in the federal government dropped from over 70 percent to 33 percent in the last ten years.[13]

In some respects this is nothing new. Americans have long held dubious views of politicians. A European traveler in 1798 noted that "disrespect to their seniors and to persons in public office seems to be strongly affected among the Americans; such at least is the humor of the rude and ill-bred among them." He said this arose from "mistaken notions of liberty," since "if ever the public office-bearers have a right to general respect" it must be those elected by the people.[14] Those American politicians who garner the most respect are the ones who stay closest to their constituents. Americans are swift to puncture the pretensions of officials who think they are cut from superior cloth. Secretary of State John Kerry's trademark interrogatory "Do you know who I am?" is rightly answered with "No, Mr. Kerry, I don't."

Even George Washington faced popular criticism. British traveler Isaac Weld noted he had seen "numbers of men, in all other points men of respectability, that have peremptorily refused even to pay [Washington] the small compliment of drinking to his health after dinner." When pressed why, they would say that they approved of General Washington, just not President Washington. Weld wrote this off to ingratitude, and concluded "It is the spirit of dissatisfaction which forms a leading trait in the character of the Americans as a people." He believed Americans would still complain even if "their public affairs were regulated by a person sent from heaven." In this respect, the American attitude toward politicians has always been "What have you done for me lately?"[15]

However, in recent years the American people seem to have turned against the system itself. The last decade has seen dramatic declines in faith in the federal government. A 2001 Gallup survey found 50 percent very or somewhat satisfied with the size and power of the federal government, and 47 percent very or somewhat dissatisfied. By 2011 only 31 percent were in the satisfied column, with 67 percent dissatisfied—and the entire twenty-point increase came in the "very dissatisfied" category.[16] An ABC News/*Washington Post* poll from December 2000 found 55 percent satisfied with the way the federal government works, 34 percent dissatisfied, and 6 percent angry. The same question in a June 2010 poll yielded only 28 percent satisfied, 45 percent dissatisfied, and 25 percent angry. In a December 2011 Gallup poll asking which would be the greatest threat to the country in the future, big government, big business, or big labor, government was the clear winner with 64 percent of responses. This number was up from 47 percent in 2002 and basically double what it was in 1970.[17]

At the most fundamental level—the level of the social contract—government legitimacy is almost nonexistent. An August 2011 Rasmussen poll found that only 17 percent of likely U.S. voters (the most politically active and aware class) agreed that "the federal government today has the consent of the governed."[18] The number saying government had consent had dropped from 23 percent the previous May, and was the lowest level ever measured by this survey. Recalling the words of the Declaration of Independence—that "governments are instituted among men, deriving their just powers from the consent of the governed" and "whenever any form of government becomes destructive to these ends, it is the right of the people to alter or to abolish it"—these are troubling statistics.

The Imperial District

Americans are also feeling more disconnected from their nation's capital and the people in it. Those who most revere Washington the general and political leader utter his name with a measure of contempt when referring to the capital. Washington, D.C., has come to symbolize an "us or them" mentality; there is no shared sense of fate, no notion that we are all in it together. As Ronald Reagan used to quip, "the nine most terrifying words in the English language are, 'I'm from the government and I'm here to help.'"

Washington, an invented city on the banks of the Potomac River, has always been a town apart. In 1908, British observer Sydney Brooks wrote the following in an essay entitled "Monarchial America":

> *The beautiful and spacious city on the banks of the Potomac is unlike any capital in Europe or any of its sister cities in America.*

> *It is an American community, doing un-American things, leading an un-American life. It lives simply for two things—society and politics. It neither talks business nor thinks it; the word conveys no more than a remote and abstract meaning to its mind. Commerce and all its banalities are refreshingly, delightfully absent. There is serenity, almost benignity, in its ordering of the routine of life. Nobody "hustles" in Washington. It is the one city on the continent where America is really at leisure.*[19]

Brooks predicted that the growing focus on social and political protocol would one day make Washington indistinguishable from the capitals of the Old World with their intrigues, endless ceremonies, and self-restraint. But a century later the notion of Washington and leisure hardly go together. Hustling has become a way of life. And the business world cannot afford to be absent from the District if it at all wants to continue. The explosion of lobbying groups and influence peddling is a natural consequence of the numerous powers Washington has arrogated to itself—taxes, regulations, policy guidance, and legal frameworks that can destroy fruitful business at the stroke of a pen. Massive federal budgets present incredible opportunities for the well connected. In some quarters the American dream is a no-bid, sole-source government contract.

Washington takes care of itself. Census data in 2011 showed that the National Capital Region edged out Silicon Valley to become the most affluent U.S. metropolitan area.[20] The typical Washington metro household earned $84,523 in 2010, compared to a national median income of $50,046.[21] Overall income in the D.C. area registered a drop of 0.8 percent, but that didn't faze government bureaucrats, whose salaries were determined by law. For federal workers, compensation jumped 3 percent in 2010 to an incredible average of $126,369.[22] A separate study showed that nationwide, "inflation-adjusted median household income fell 6.7 percent" between June 2009 and June 2011.[23] Figures like this feed the perception that government personnel are no longer public servants but a self-serving, self-sustaining, and remote privileged class.

Other measures confirmed that good times are rolling inside the Beltway. Unemployment in the D.C. area in August 2011 was 6.1 percent, according to the Bureau of Labor Statistics. This wasn't the lowest rate in the country, an honor that went to oil-booming Bismarck, North Dakota, at 3 percent. However, Washington's rate was the best of the ten largest U.S. metropolitan areas and far below the national unemployment rate of 9.1 percent. Millions of Americans have suffered with home mortgage problems, but there has been less of a housing crisis in Washington. The Zillow home price index showed home values went up 2.9 percent in the District in 2010–2011 while nationwide the average home value declined 4.5 percent. The average Washington home was valued at more than twice the national average and even more than homes in the New York City metropolitan area. And an August 2011 Gallup survey of confidence in the economy found that in all fifty states the majority view was that things were getting worse, while in D.C., 60 percent believed that the economy was getting better.[24]

The image of Washingtonians prospering while the rest of the country struggles sends a troubling message. There is no reason for the city's outsized prosperity other than the federal government. Washington has no important manufacturing base, it isn't a trade hub, and its agriculture is composed of weekend farmers' markets. Washington exists to collect and redistribute national income and make the country's rules. When such a city becomes the wealthiest in the country, there is a problem.

Public regard for national political institutions is at a low ebb. Government is understood to be gridlocked, broken, and under the sway of special interests. Politicians are seen as isolated, out of touch, and tone deaf to the concerns of the suffering mass of people. Across the political spectrum, confidence in the future is low and frustration is rising. Americans are anxious for some signs that Washington policy makers understand their fears and the scope of the problems facing the country. In a time of austerity, they want shared sacrifice. In an era of increasing division, Americans want more teamwork. As the American dream withers, people want public-spirited leadership that will put the Land of the Free back on the road to prosperity. But instead, Washington, D.C., takes care of itself, like imperial Rome looting its provinces. It's no wonder the barbarians are getting restless.

The Growing Political Divide

The general decline in perceptions of government legitimacy is bad enough. Add to that the growing political schism in the country and the situation seems grimmer. The United States is a deeply divided polity in which cleavages have become sharper and rhetoric more heated, and whose politics has taken on the character of a blood sport.

The center is not holding. A 2011 Gallup poll showed that among those with party affiliation, the percentage of self-identified Republican conservatives and Democratic liberals is increasing while moderates in both parties are declining. Nationally, conservatives were the largest group, with 41 percent; 36 percent self-identified as moderate and 21 percent as liberal.[25]

The contending groups have fewer shared frames of reference than in the past. Technology has contributed to the development of niche media. The era of the Big Three television networks and relatively few large, respected newspapers and news magazines has been succeeded by the rise of cable television, talk radio, and the Internet. Whereas in the past people with a strong political bent would subscribe to magazines or newsletters that arrived periodically with information that spoke to their viewpoint, today they have instant access to virtually unlimited amounts of information to massage their biases. All points of view—from the most respectable to the most inane, from the reasonable to the crackpot—have online news sources, blogs, bulletin boards, social media pages, ebooks, and preferred advocates to cheer them on in the arena.

A September 2010 study from the Pew Center found that "Ideology continues to be closely associated with people's choice of certain news sources." Those who get information from Rush Limbaugh, Glenn Beck, or Sean Hannity are twice as conservative as the nation at large, while those who gravitate to Jon Stewart, Stephen Colbert, Keith Olbermann, and Rachel Maddow are twice as liberal.[26] Common frames of reference are fading, and a generalized understanding of the American experience is being broken by the severity of the contending forces. Jon Stewart wrongly mocked Fox News viewers for being "consistently" the most "uninformed" news consumers, yet increasing numbers of young liberals rely on his explicitly satirical and comedic show for what they consider to be news and information.[27] Keith Olbermann arrogated to himself the role of declaring daily the "worst person in the world," with the common denominator apparently being those who did not agree with him.[28] All sides now come to the debate armed with their own facts, their own history, their own causes, and a take-no-prisoners attitude that is certain to render the outcome of public policy discussions failed before they begin. It begs the question, if so many people despise each other so thoroughly, so completely, what sense does it make for them to continue their journey together?

The Congress reflects the country's polarization. In the late nineteenth century there was a strong partisan and regional division on Capitol Hill, which was primarily the residue of the Civil War. Party polarization began to decline gradually in the early twentieth century, then rapidly after the First World War. In the middle of the century, the partisan lines were blurred in Congress due to a leftward drift of the Republican Party and rightward drift of southern Democrats. But this era of cooperation began to break down after the 1960s. According to a study by Keith T. Poole of the

University of California, San Diego, political moderates "virtually disappeared during the thirty years between the 93rd [1973–1975] and 108th [2003–2005] Congresses and the parties have pulled apart. In the early 1970s there was considerable overlap of the two political parties. In the past ten years that overlap has almost completely disappeared." The percentage of "party unity" votes increased from around 70 percent to around 95 percent, and the proportion of moderates in both parties has dropped to around 10 percent. By the time of the 110th Congress (2007–2009), voting in Congress became "almost purely one-dimensional—[the liberal/conservative] dimension accounts for about 93 percent of roll call voting choices in the 110th House and Senate—and the two parties are increasingly polarized." [29] It is the highest level of political polarization in 120 years; things are worse today than in the days when veterans of the Union and Confederate armies maneuvered against each other in Congress as they had on the battlefield, with the same warlike spirit, just armed with different weapons.

Views of the chief executive have also become more divisive in recent years. The use of the expression "not *my* president"—which became established during Lyndon Johnson's presidency (chiefly among leftist dissenters in his own party)—soared after the contested 2001 election of George W. Bush.[30] The slogan continued into the Obama administration, and in February 2012 the *Washington Post* ran a headline announcing "Obama: The most polarizing president. Ever." The *Post* referred to a report by Gallup that found that Barack Obama was the most divisive president in sixty years of polling.[31] For the first three years of his presidency the partisan divide in Mr. Obama's approval ratings was the highest of any on record, going back to the Truman administration. In 2011, the gap between his approval ratings by party was 68 percent, the highest for any third-year president.

The reasons for the division are easy to discern. During the 2008 presidential campaign, Mr. Obama promised to heal the partisan breach. He said he would be a unifier, that he would reach across party lines, that he would forge consensus. Once he took office, however, armed with a hard-left agenda and backed by a supermajority in Congress, the arrogance of power overwhelmed the better angels of his nature. Those who questioned his policies were labeled extremists, or worse. Dissent was smacked down, Congress rammed through his contentious programs, and Democrats were punished for their conceit with a "shellacking" in the 2010 midterm elections.

Yet President Obama did not cause the division, he simply exacerbated a trend toward disunity that had been developing for years. While the Gallup data show that Mr. Obama had the most polarized first three years in office, they also revealed that George W. Bush held the top three slots for most divisive presidential years ever, occurring 2004–2007. If nothing else, this showed that the partisan antipathy was mutual. More alarming is the fact that this is a recent phenomenon; eight of the top-ten most-divided years have occurred in an unbroken line from 2004 to the present.

The problem goes much deeper than Messrs. Obama and Bush, and the decline in political legitimacy goes beyond the executive branch. As noted earlier, regard for Congress has been on a nosedive for the past ten years. Disapproval ratings for the U.S. Supreme Court are near record highs as well. According to a Gallup report released in September 2011, the general sense of satisfaction over how the country is being governed dropped from 59 percent in 2003 to a historic low of 19 percent.[32] These data demonstrate a growing undercurrent of discontent. The gulf is deep, and growing deeper.

The severity of the split reflects the centralization of political power over recent decades, the drive for one-size-fits-all government, the rash of increasingly complex and controlling economic regulations, and the institutionalized divisions championed by multiculturalists in the name of "diversity." People are forced into all-or-nothing contests because those are the stakes the system has set. In the past the consequences of failure by politicians were tempered by the fact that the effects would be limited—government had less power, thus was less of a threat. But now every dispute takes on a life-or-death quality. Rhetoric has become outsized and fantastic. A permanent war-room mentality has taken over, not just in electoral politics but also in lawmaking, policy making, and every facet of public life. The division has spread throughout the culture, in entertainment, education, and religion. It has hardened and embittered the two sides of the struggle and rendered the government, if not the society, dysfunctional.

Preserving the Dream

America is beset by powerful forces, the effects of which can only be guessed. The rise of foreign competitor states, the decline in relative economic power, and the deepening division in American public life all point to an unsettled future. The country has faced such times before; in 1859, as the United States stood on the verge of tearing itself apart, Abraham Lincoln warned that "the principles of Jefferson are the definitions and axioms of free society. And yet they are denied, and evaded, with no small show of success. . . . Soberly, it is now no child's play to save the principles of Jefferson from total overthrow in this nation."[33]

One scenario looks to a time when the United States has become a shadow of its former self, with a permanently weakened economy and scant global influence. The country would be overwhelmed with debts it could not pay and rising conflicts over the remaining, shrinking public resources. The world would be a more violent place absent the steadying presence of U.S. power, and other countries would attempt to either fill or exploit the vacuum. The most motivated people would leave the United States, either trying to preserve their wealth, escape growing domestic discord, or simply seek opportunities in countries that still had them. They would find those places where the ideals that made America what it was are fresh—the greener pastures where they could flourish as they might have, had the United States remained true to its founding principles. It would be a world with clusters of Americans, the preserving remnant, living as émigrés in their adopted lands and thinking wistfully of the past, mourning the destruction of the New Jerusalem. They would take the spirit of the people with them, leaving behind a United States without Americans.

Another scenario foresees the division between the two competing and irreconcilable worldviews in the United States growing so great that it becomes formalized. There are undercurrents of this notion on the right and the left, a sense that it is simply not worth the fight any more. Proponents of this view think of how much easier it would be not to have to contend with the other side, which they see as irrational, dangerous, and unstable. At some point the increasing demands and recriminations, the zero-sum competition over centralized power, the evolution of two (or more) distinct cultures would lead to the realization that the house should no longer remain undivided. A point would arrive when each side says to the other, "We don't owe you anything, we don't want to live under your laws, we reject any claim you have on our lives and liberties." Those with separate visions for America would peacefully and constitutionally part ways and chart their own courses in new experiments in liberty, under their own banners. They would, to quote the Declaration of Independence, "dissolve the political bands which have connected them with another and . . . assume among the powers of the earth, the separate and equal station to which the Laws of Nature and of Nature's God entitle them."

A third scenario requires a call to action. It seeks to recapture the American spirit and consciously embrace the American identity to find common ground. Accept a shared history and common vision for the future based on American ideals. Tone down the disputes that ravage the body politic. Heat up the melting pot and stop drawing lines that divide the people. Stop seeking new ways to create differences and calling it a virtue. End the endless fighting over the same supposed moral high ground that has left it a burned-over hill. Rediscover the positive virtues of America and harness the natural optimism of a free people. The best days can still be ahead.

Renewing America first requires personal initiative. The U.S. Citizenship and Immigration Services advises applicants that "citizenship offers many benefits and equally important responsibilities." These are listed as: supporting and defending the Constitution; staying informed of community issues; participating in the democratic process; respecting and obeying the law; respecting the rights, beliefs, and opinions of others; participating in local communities; paying taxes; serving on juries; and defending the country if the need should arise. However, many Americans do few if any of these things, including voting and paying taxes. People need to be more active in their local governments and nongovernment civic institutions. This involves not just voting, but volunteering for civic activities, even standing for office. There is a great need in the country for citizen-politicians to dilute the influence of the entrenched political class. America is best served when outstanding Americans share their gifts with their communities and the country.

People should also find ways to support local institutions such as fire departments, the police, hospitals, retirement homes, religious institutions, and other pillars of community life. Volunteering for military service is another way to serve the country, renewing the covenant made by the minutemen and the Revolution's soldiers, sailors and Marines that there would always be Americans ready to devote their lives to the maintenance of freedom.

Americans need to refresh their perspectives. Most young people have been raised in relative affluence and security, and the harsh oppression or lack of opportunity experienced by their immigrant ancestors is generations removed or an academic exercise. Youngsters should understand that the freedoms they benefit from are not enjoyed by the majority of the world's population. Children of the fourth or later generations, without immigrant relations still alive, are at most danger of taking the American way of life for granted.

Exposure to what it feels like to experience the absence of freedom—the specific emotions of need, and economic and religious oppression—requires personal effort, such as inviting foreign-born individuals into our homes and schools, or travelling to other countries. It requires researching, telling, and retelling our own families' histories of coming to America. And most importantly, it requires a value judgment: a decision to tell our youth that life in America is indeed better than life in other countries, and that most of our ancestors literally voted with their feet to give us the incredible birthright we enjoy. In this way they can grow to understand their families'—and America's—journey toward freedom.

Girls and young women should be encouraged to appreciate that American society supports a fluidity in gender roles that yields them opportunities for a wider and richer life than they could enjoy nearly anywhere else on the planet. They are uniquely free to pursue education, to compete with men for jobs, to wear modest or immodest garb, and to self-determine how and when they build their families. Many modern Americans can identify a family matriarch or two who actively chose to immigrate to America in order to embrace these freedoms for herself and her family, and it would benefit our daughters to dwell on these family heroes.

Passing the torch to future generations is critical for America to survive. "Freedom is never more than one generation away from extinction," Ronald Reagan observed. "We didn't pass it to our children in the bloodstream. It must be fought for, protected, and handed on for them to do the same, or one day we will spend our sunset years telling our children and our children's children what it was once like in the United States where men were free."[34]

Of the many concerns about American public education, one issue that is particularly pressing is the failure to provide basic education about civics and United States history. The results of a 2010 study of the National Assessment of Educational Progress revealed that "12 percent of seniors are proficient in U.S. history, while only 24 percent measure up in civics."[35] According to former Supreme Court Justice Sandra Day O'Connor, who is heading an initiative on this matter, civics education is not required in over half the states in the union.[36] This flies in the face of the purpose of public school education, which is to create citizens able to participate in self-governance. If young people fail to understand the structure, role, and interaction of local, state, and federal government, and their rights and responsibilities within these social contracts, they will necessarily be less committed to maintaining them. Most likely, they will also be less inclined to participate and more willing to accept a handout, since the source of government largesse remains unclear. And even when civics and U.S. history are taught, parental engagement cannot end at the classroom door. The content of textbooks requires active involvement, particularly when textbook publishers routinely dismiss or debase national myths and heroes.

In general, the effort to rebuild America requires a positive vision and an optimistic outlook. The Englishman John Duncan, who two hundred years ago warned his countrymen against unrealistic dreams of easy prosperity in the New World, nevertheless recognized the potential of America. "A grand experiment in politics and religion is there going forward—an experiment which, if successful, will be productive of unestimated happiness to the human race," he wrote. "Of their future destiny and influence we can say nothing; but he is not a friend to his species, who does not wish well to the United States."[37] The country was not predestined to prosper; it did so because of the choices made, from the earliest days, to nurture the spirits of liberty and community that allowed those who set their sights on America and its ideals to live and work and flourish in the manner of their choosing. The stewardship of the country and, more importantly, of the ideal, requires each generation to recognize, honor, and carry forward the grand experiment of the first new nation. The American spirit will not die. It is the best within us, the spark of genius, of inspiration, and of faith. So long as that spirit abides, there will always be Americans.

NOTES

Chapter 1

1. William Damon, "American Amnesia," *Defining Ideas*, July 1, 2011. Dr. Damon's essay was based on his book, *Failing Liberty 101: How We Are Leaving Young Americans Unprepared for Citizenship in a Free Society* (Stanford, CA: Hoover Institution Press, 2011).

2. James Kirkup, "Muslims must embrace our British values, David Cameron says," *The Telegraph* (February 5, 2011).

3. Andrew Porter, "David Cameron: migration threatens our way of life," *The Telegraph* (April 13, 2011).

4. Chris Pollard, "John Cleese: London is no longer English city," *The Sun* (September 4, 2011).

5. Matthew Clark, "Germany's Angela Merkel: Multiculturalism has 'utterly failed,'" *The Christian Science Monitor* (October 17, 2010).

6. Quoted in Soeren Kern, "Angry Turk's Message for Europe: 'We Are Coming,'" *Pundicity* (March 16, 2012).

7. "France's Sarkozy: Multiculturalism a failure," *Reuters* (February 11, 2011).

8. James S. Robbins, "The Oslo Terrorist in His Own Words: Bomber Predicted 'Europe soon will burn once again,'" *The Washington Times* (July 23, 2011).

9. "The life and death of French gunman Mohamed Merah," *The Los Angeles Times* (March 22, 2012).

Chapter 2

1. Objectivists and Ayn Rand aficionados may particularly be interested in the note on the top left corner of the Waldseemüller map that reads, "Many have thought to be an invention what the famous Poet [Virgil] said, that 'a land lies beyond the stars, beyond the paths of the year and the sun, where Atlas the heaven-bearer turns on his shoulder the axis of the world set with blazing stars;' but now, at last, it proves clearly to have been true. It is, in fact, the land discovered by the King of Castile's captain, Columbus, and by Americo Vesputius, men of great and excellent talent, of which the greater part lies under the path of the year and sun, and between the tropics but extending nonetheless to about nineteen degrees beyond Capricorn toward the Antarctic pole beyond the paths of the year and the sun. Wherein, indeed, a greater amount of gold is to be found than of any other metal."

2. George Berkeley, *A proposal for the better supplying of churches in our foreign plantations* (London: H. Woodfall, 1725), 17.

3. James Gibson, *A journal of the late siege by the troops from North America* (London: J. Newberry, 1747), 43. The author further notes, "By these Means true Religion and Virtue may gradually succeed in the Place of Superstition and Idolatry; and Humanity, Faith and good Morals, instead of Cruelty, Ignorance and Jesuitical Principles, destructive of all the former."

4. Josiah Rucker, *A Brief Essay on the Advantages and Disadvantages which Respectively Attend France and Great Britain, with Regard to Trade*, 3rd ed. (London: T. Trye, 1753), 102–103. Rucker argued, years before Burke, that such mercantilist measures would harm Britain by cutting more expensive British bar iron out of the market, hence "this Difference in the Price is in fact a Bounty given by yourselves for the Encouragement

of Iron-Manufactures in America." He called it "an astonishing Instance of the Ignorance and Infatuation of the English in regard to their own Interest."

5. *The Scots Magazine*, vol. 3 (June 1741), 274.

6. *The London Magazine, or, Gentleman's Monthly Intelligencer* (August 1755), 382.

7. John Shebbeare, *Letters on the English Nation, by Batista Angeloni, a Jesuit*, who resided many years in London (London, 1755), xix. The highest-ranking American officer accompanying Braddock's force was Colonel George Washington, who assumed command when Braddock was slain near Fort Duquesne in July 1755.

8. H. W. Brand, on "Think Tank with Ben Wattenberg" (May 29, 2003).

9. Sherman Edwards and Peter Stone, *1776: A Musical Play* (New York: Viking Press, 1970).

10. Lord Dunmore, to the Earl of Dartmouth, secretary of state for the colonies, December 24, 1774. In *Documentary History of Dunmore's War*, R. G. Thwaites and L. P. Kellogg, eds. (Madison: Wisconsin Historical Society, 1905), 371–372.

11. Arthur Aikin, *The Annual Review, and History of Literature*, vol. 4 (London: Longman, Hurst, Rees and Orme, 1806), 276.

12. Francois VI, Duc de la Rochefoucault-Liancourt, *Travels through the United States of North America, the country of the Iroquois, and Upper Canada, in the years 1795, 1796, and 1797; with an authentic account of Lower Canada* (London: T. Davison, 1799), 107.

13. "The American Character," *The Literary magazine, and American register for 1804*, vol. 2, Charles Brockden Brown, ed., (Philadelphia: J. Conrad & Co., 1804), 254.

14. "The American Character," 256.

15. American State Papers, in *The Monthly Anthology and Boston Review*, vol. 4 (1807), 39.

16. See James S. Robbins, "Fantastic Voyage," *National Review Online* (October 10, 2005) and "Celebrate America on Columbus Day," *The Wash-*

ington Times (October 7, 2011), from which the following was in part adapted.

17. Simon Willard Jr., *The Columbian Union, containing general and particular explanations of government, and the Columbian Constitution, being an amendment to the constitution of the United States* (Albany, 1814), 116, 120.

18. Jean-Jacques Ampère, *Promenade en Amérique; États-Unis, Cuba, Mexique* (Paris: Michel Lévy Frères, 1860), 8.

19. Richard Thornton, "Native Americans and fiscal reformers say, 'Goodbye Columbus!'" *The Examiner* (October 10, 2011).

20. See *The Course of Study: A Monthly Publication for Teachers and Parents* (Chicago: The Chicago Institute, July 1900), 255.

Chapter 3

1. See the author's "Obama and America's Decline," *The Washington Times* (November 9, 2010). Some passages here are adapted from that essay. For the general discussion of American exceptionalism, see *inter alia* Seymour Martin Lipset, *American Exceptionalism: A Double-Edged Sword* (New York: W.W. Norton and Co., 1996); Godfrey Hodgson, *The Myth of American Exceptionalism* (New Haven: Yale University Press, 2009); and Andrew J. Bacevich, *The Limits of Power: The End of American Exceptionalism* (New York: Henry Holt and Company, 2008), as well as other works cited below.

2. Thucydides, *The Peloponnesian War,* trans. Rex Warner (New York: Penguin Books, 1982), 143–151.

3. Margaret Thatcher, speech at Hoover Institution Lunch, Washington, D.C., March 8, 1991.

4. Ronald Reagan, "The Shining City Upon a Hill," speech to the first Conservative Political Action Conference, January 25, 1974.

5. The inspiration for this passage was in the book of Matthew 5:14–16: "Ye are the light of the world. A city that is set on an hill cannot be hid. Neither do men light a candle, and put it under a bushel, but on

a candlestick; and it giveth light unto all that are in the house. Let your light so shine before men, that they may see your good works, and glorify your Father which is in heaven." (KJV).

6. Winthrop's views of the Indians echo Psalm 2:8: "Ask of me, and I shall give thee the heathen for thine inheritance, and the uttermost parts of the earth for thy possession." (KJV). His take on the 1634 smallpox epidemic is similar to viewing the AIDS epidemic as the product of divine judgment, or Hurricane Katrina as an example of God's wrath against the "den of sin" of New Orleans.

7. Quoted in Calvin Coolidge, "The Inspiration of the Declaration of Independence," speech in Philadelphia to mark the 150th Anniversary of the Declaration of Independence, July 5, 1926.

8. George Washington, "First Inaugural Address," April 30, 1789.

9. Quoted in James Ford Rhodes, *History of the United States,* vol. 3 (London: The Macmillan Co., 1910), 82–83.

10. Georg Wilhelm Friedrich Hegel, *The Philosophy of History* (Barnes & Noble Books, 2004), 93.

11. Quoted in Everett H. Emerson, *American Literature, 1764-1789: The Revolutionary Years* (Madison: University of Wisconsin Press, 1977), 277.

12. Thomas Jefferson to George Rogers Clark, December 25, 1780, in Julian P. Bond et al., eds., *The Papers of Thomas Jefferson,* vol. 4 (Princeton, NJ: Princeton University Press, 1950), 237–238.

13. Thomas Jefferson to Dr. Joseph Priestley, January 29, 1804, in *Jefferson, Letters,* Merrill D. Peterson, ed. (New York: Literary Classics of the United States, 1984), 1142.

14. Thomas Jefferson to James Madison, April 27, 1809, in *The Writings of Thomas Jefferson,* vol. 12, Albert Ellery Bergh, ed. (Washington, D.C.: Thomas Jefferson Memorial Association of the United States, 1905), 277.

15. Thomas Jefferson to William Ludlow, September 6, 1824, in *The Writings of Thomas Jefferson,* vol. 16 (Washington, D.C.: Thomas Jefferson Memorial Association of the United States, 1905), 75.

16. There is a direct conceptual line from Jefferson's Empire of Liberty to what would later be called the "neoconservative" model of liberating people abroad who were crushed under the weight of dictatorships.

17. Texas was an independent country that had split off from Mexico in 1836 and joined the United States on December 29, 1845. The treaty with Mexico did not acknowledge this (because Mexico had never acknowledged Texas' independence), but simply noted that the border with the United States was set at the Rio Grande.

18. Henry Wadsworth Longfellow Dana, "'Sail on, O Ship of State!' How Longfellow Came to Write These Lines 100 Years Ago," *The Colby Quarterly* (February 1950).

19. The slogan "Fifty-Four Forty or Fight!" was coined in 1846 and referred to the northernmost American claims to the Oregon Territory, at latitude 54°40' north. The border was ultimately set at 49°, without a fight. The 1854 Gadsden Purchase added an additional almost 30,000 square miles to what would become southern Arizona and southwestern New Mexico. The area was acquired to facilitate construction of a transcontinental railway.

20. *American Review: A Whig Journal*, vol. 6 (New York: Wiley and Putnam, October 1847), 338.

21. Robert Vincent Remini, *Henry Clay: Statesman for the Union* (New York: W.W. Norton and Co., 1991), 221–224. Note that Clay later opposed the war with Mexico and was not a proponent of Manifest Destiny. The "great compromiser" did not fit easily into an ideological box.

22. John Quincy Adams, address on July 4, 1821, in *Library of the World's Best Literature, Ancient and Modern*, vol. 1, Charles Dudley Warner, ed. (New York: J. A. Hill & Company, 1902), 142.

23. The United States had long fought counterinsurgencies against American Indians. The Second Seminole War (1835–1842) in particular was a brutal pacification campaign whose lessons had to be relearned several times. See James S. Robbins, *Last in Their Class: Custer, Pickett and the Goats of West Point* (New York: Encounter Books, 2006), Chapter 4.

24. See James S. Robbins, *This Time We Win: Revisiting the Tet Offensive* (New York: Encounter Books, 2010).

25. This was known as the Kirkpatrick Doctrine after the thesis developed by Jeanne Kirkpatrick in her November 1979 essay in *Commentary*, "Dictatorships and Double Standards." She later served as Ronald Reagan's Ambassador to the United Nations.

26. Francis Fukuyama, *The End of History and the Last Man* (New York: The Free Press, 1992).

27. Henry Demarest Lloyd, *The Swiss democracy: The study of a sovereign people* (London: T. Fisher Unwin, 1908). In this book, Lloyd coined the expression "laboratory of democracy" to apply to the Swiss Confederation. Others used it favorably to describe the British Empire, and Theodore Roosevelt used it to describe the state of Wisconsin.

28. Brandeis dissent in *New State Ice Co. v. Liebmann*, 285 U.S. 262 (1932).

29. Cf. Rael Jean Isaac and Erich Isaac, *The Coercive Utopians: Social Deception by America's Power Players* (Chicago: Regnery Gateway, 1984).

30. The expression "more perfect union" in the preamble to the Constitution refers specifically to a better government than that under the Articles of Confederation, not to a Platonic perfect form.

31. Brett Stephens, "The President of Contempt," *The Wall Street Journal* (October 4, 2011).

32. In this case the court upheld the right of Old Order Amish children to leave public schools after the eighth grade, in part as recognition of their religious beliefs, but also because the Amish have "a history of three centuries as an identifiable religious sect and a long history as a successful and self-sufficient segment of American society."

33. Carl Schurz, *Writings*, vol. 1 (New York: Putnam, 1913), 5–8.

34. Max Lerner, *America as a Civilization* (New York: Simon & Schuster, 1957), 65.

Chapter 4

1. Carl Schurz, *Writings*, vol. 1 (New York: Putnam, 1913), 5–8.
2. Quoted in *Niles' Register* (September 6, 1828), 23.

3. Jefferson to Roger C. Weightman, June 24, 1826, *The Writings of Thomas Jefferson*, vol. 16 (Washington, D.C.: Thomas Jefferson Memorial Association of the United States, 1905), 182. In this, his final letter, Mr. Jefferson hoped that the legacy of the Declaration of Independence would be "the signal of arousing men to burst the chains under which monkish ignorance and superstition had persuaded them to bind themselves, and to assume the blessings and security of self-government. That form which we have substituted, restores the free right to the unbounded exercise of reason and freedom of opinion."

4. Harris Interactive poll, *E Pluribus Unum: A Study of Americans' Views of National Identity*, commissioned for the Bradley Project on American National Identity (June 2008).

5. Ayn Rand, "Man's Rights," in *Capitalism, the Unknown Ideal* (New York: Signet, 1966).

6. Quoted in John P. Roche, "Founding Fathers: Tough, Talented," King Features Syndicate, (July 3, 1976).

7. Thomas Jefferson disagreed. Calvin's "religion was demonism," he wrote. "If ever man worshiped a false God, he did. The being described in his five points is . . . a demon of malignant spirit. It would be more pardonable to believe in no God at all, than to blaspheme him by the atrocious attributes of Calvin." *Thomas Jefferson Works*, vol. 4, 363.

8. Thomas Hobbes, *Leviathan*, J. C. A. Gaskin, ed. (Oxford: Oxford University Press, 1996).

9. The story of the *Sea Venture* was purportedly the inspiration for William Shakespeare's *The Tempest*.

10. Caleb Johnson, *Here Shall I Die Ashore: Stephen Hopkins, Bermuda Castaway, Jamestown Survivor, and Mayflower Pilgrim* (Xlibris Publishing, 2007).

11. From Bradford's Journal, in *Colonial American Writing*, Roy Harvey Pearce, ed. (New York: Rinehart and Company, 1950), 34.

12. Roche, "Founding Fathers."

13. Edmund Burke, "On Conciliation with America," a speech delivered in the House of Commons, March 22, 1775, in *The Works of the Right Hon. Edmund Burke*, vol. 1 (London: Holdsworth and Ball, 1834), 188.

14. As used in the 1997 Apple Computer advertising campaign "Think Different."

15. Randolph wasn't done yet. In 1691 he was appointed surveyor of customs for all of North America, but met with little success trying to enforce English trade laws.

16. *London Public Advertiser* (March 15, 1775).

17. *London Evening Post* (August 26, 1775).

18. Burke, "On Conciliation with America."

19. Richard Henry Spencer, "The Carlyle House and Its Associations—Braddock's Headquarters—Here the Colonial Governors met in Council, April, 1755," *William and Mary College Quarterly Historical Magazine*, vol. 18 no. 1 (July 1909), 9.

20. Roche, "Founding Fathers."

21. John Adams to H. Niles, February 13, 1818.

22. Burke, "On Conciliation with America."

Chapter 5

1. "President Obama's Remarks on the Homeowner Affordability and Stability Plan," *The New York Times* (February 18, 2009).

2. It turned out that Mr. Santelli was right about the mortgage relief plan. Mr. Obama's soaring rhetoric aside, the administration's mortgage relief and affordability plans turned out to be expensive failures. See Kristin Roberts and Stacy Kaper, "Out of Their Depth," *National Journal*, March 22, 2012.

3. Quoted in David Weigel, "Imagining a World Without the Tea Party," *Slate* (October 31, 2011).

4. E. J. Dionne Jr., "What Our Declaration Really Said," *The Washington Post* (July 3, 2011).

5. See the author's "The Media Ride of Sarah Palin," *The Washington Times* (June 7, 2011).

6. *London General Evening Post* (January 1, 1774), 3.

7. *London Craftsman or Say's Weekly Journal* (January 29, 1774), 1.

8. *Boston Weekly Magazine*, vol. 3 (1805), 163.

9. *The New England Farmer*, vol. 4 (1826), 243.

10. James Hawkes, *A retrospect of the Boston tea-party: with a memoir of George R. T. Hewes*, (New York: S. Eliss, 1834).

11. Hawkes, *A retrospect of the Boston tea-party*, 8.

12. Usage data according to Google Ngrams.

13. Eugene Robinson, "What's behind the Tea Party's ire?" *The Washington Post* (November 2, 2010). See also James W. Caesar and John York, "Blaming It All on the Tea Party," *Commentary* (July 15, 2011). The article lists the "seven deadly sins" of the Tea Party.

14. See the author's "The Race Card Canard," *The Washington Times* (March 23, 2010).

15. Lydia Saad, "Tea Partiers Are Fairly Mainstream in Their Demographics," *Gallup Politics* (April 5, 2010).

16. Kate Zernike and Megan Thee-Brenan, "Poll Finds Tea Party Backers Wealthier and More Educated," *The New York Times* (April 14, 2010).

17. Susan Page and Naomi Jagoda, "What is the Tea Party? A growing state of mind," *USA Today* (July 8, 2010).

18. Quoted in the English publication *The Bee: or Literary Weekly Intelligencer*, James Anderson, ed., vol. 18 (1794), 330. The editor added that "In the end of this awful year, and looking forward to another, I give [Washington's words] as a Christmas offering to the world, and am not afraid of its being ill received by any rational and well intentioned man under the canopy of Heaven."

19. An earlier use of the term was the title of a 1703 English play, *The Patriot, or the Italian Conspiracy*.

20. John Adams, *A Defense of the Constitutions of the United States* (Philadelphia: Budd and Bartram, 1797), xvii.

21. *The Works of Sallust*, T. Gordon, ed. (London: Woodward and Peele, 1744).

22. "The True Patriot," *Gentleman's Magazine* (June 1734), 327.

23. *The Grub-Street Journal* (January 10, 1733). The editorial noted the term patriot generally means "some eminent subject who stands up in defense of the laws and liberties of his own native country, in opposition to those who join with courtiers in pillaging it, and bringing it under tyrannical oppression."

24. Viscount Henry St. John Bolingbroke, "The Idea of a Patriot King," 1749.

25. "The Patriot King, or George the Third," *London Annual Register* (January 1, 1761).

26. Paul Johnson, *A History of the American People (*New York: HarperCollins, 1997), 142. Johnson averred that Samuel Johnson's statement was a direct reaction to the Boston Tea Party, i.e., that these were the original scoundrels. However, the Tea Party was several years prior to the statement and, as noted below, under much different circumstances.

27. James Boswell, *Boswell's Life of Johnson* (London: John Murray, 1847), 446. Another case has been made that Johnson was referring to John Stuart, 3rd Earl of Bute, another dubious "patriot minister."

28. Quoted in Stephen Miller, *Three Deaths and Enlightenment Thought: Hume, Johnson, Marat* (Lewisburg, PA: Bucknell University Press, 2001), 76. This brings to mind comedian Lenny Bruce's comments about Lyndon Johnson's difficulties pronouncing the word "negro" correctly once he took up the cause of civil rights.

29. Samuel Johnson, *The Patriot: Addressed to the electors of Great Britain* (Dublin: Octavo, 1775), 17.

30. Data on frequency of word usage from Google Ngrams. "Patriotism" has generally been twice as commonly used as "patriot," but the two words track the same pattern of post–Civil War decline.

31. "PATRIOT" is an acronym for the Uniting (and) Strengthening America (by) Providing Appropriate Tools Required (to) Intercept (and) Obstruct Terrorism. Regardless of the law's value in combating terrorism,

it is one of the most obnoxiously named pieces of legislation in American history, and solidified the contemporary practice of naming every major piece of legislation in a way that renders a trite acronym.

32. Lymari Morales, "One in Three Americans 'Extremely Patriotic,'" *Gallup Politics* (July 2, 2010). Also cf. the author's "The Patriotism Gap," *The Washington Times* (July 7, 2010).

33. "COMMUNISTS: Rain Check on Revolution," *Time* (May 30, 1938).

34. Nancy Pelosi speech on the U.S. Capitol steps, March 22, 2012.

35. Andreas Madestam and David Yanagizawa-Drott, "Shaping the Nation: The Effect of Fourth of July on Political Preferences and Behavior in the United States," Kennedy School of Government Working Paper No. RWP12-034 (November 1, 2011). See also the author's "Patriotism on Parade," *The Washington Times* (July 1, 2011), from which this section is adapted.

Chapter 6

1. Quoted in *The Survey* (May 1941), 139.

2. "Does the US Constitution Still Work for 21st Century America?" Penn Schoen Berland Poll, Aspen Ideas Festival (July 9, 2010).

3. John P. Roche, "The Founding Fathers: A Reform Caucus in Action," *The American Political Science Review*, vol. 55, Issue 4 (December 1961), 799–816.

4. In full, the First Amendment reads, "Congress shall make no law respecting an establishment of religion, or prohibiting the free exercise thereof; or abridging the freedom of speech, or of the press; or the right of the people peaceably to assemble, and to petition the government for a redress of grievances."

5. Alexander Hamilton to Gouverneur Morris, January 27, 1802.

6. "Startling Lack of Constitutional Knowledge Revealed in First-Ever National Poll," National Constitution Center, on poll taken September 17–23, 1997.

7. "Pomp, and a Little Circumstance," *The New York Times* (January 4, 2011).

8. Penn Schoen Berland Poll.

9. *Marbury v. Madison,* 5 U.S. 137 (1803).

10. Jeffrey M. Jones, "Supreme Court Approval Rating Dips to 46%," *Gallup Politics* (October 3, 2011).

11. Kaiser Health Tracking Poll, Kaiser Family Foundation (March 2012).

12. Mark Penn, "Poll Shows People Support Checks and Balances, But Want More Limits on Supreme Court Justices," *The Huffington Post* (July 9, 2010).

13. Alesh Houdek, "Has a Harvard Professor Mapped Out the Next Step for Occupy Wall Street?" *The Atlantic* (November 16, 2011).

Chapter 7

1. "Fifth Annual MetLife Study of the American Dream: The Do It Yourself Dream," MetLife (2011).

2. James Truslow Adams, *The Epic of America* (Garden City, NY: Garden City Books, 1933), 412.

3. For a detailed discussion, see Jim Cullen, *The American Dream: A Short History of an Idea that Shaped a Nation* (New York: Oxford University Press, 2003).

4. J. Hector St. John de Crèvecoeur, *Letters from an American Farmer/ by J. Hector St. John de Crèvecoeur, reprinted from the original ed., with a prefatory note by W. P. Trent and introduction by Ludwig Lewisohn* (New York: Fox, Duffield, and Company, 1904), 55–56. For an extended discussion of the theme of the American as a "new man," see James Truslow Adams, *The American* (New York: Charles Scribner's Sons, 1944). Also D. W. Brogan, *The American Character* (New York: Time Incorporated, 1962).

5. The following section is adapted from James S. Robbins, "Pilgrim Parable," *National Review Online* (November 27, 2002).

6. Edward Winslow, quoted in *The Puritan Tradition in America: 1620–1730*, Alden T. Vaughan, ed. (Hanover, NH: University Press of New England, 1972), 51.

7. William Bradford, quoted in *Colonial Prose and Poetry: The Transplanting of Culture, 1607–1650*, William Peterfield Trent, and Benjamin Willis Wells, eds. (New York: Thomas Y. Crowell & Co., 1901), 47.

8. In Alexander Young, *Chronicles of the Pilgrim fathers of the colony of Plymouth: from 1602–1625* (Boston: Charles C. Little and James Brown, 1844), 264–265.

9. Ibid.

10. Bradford, in *Colonial Prose and Poetry*, 48.

11. Ibid.

12. Ibid.

13. Max Weber, *The Protestant Ethic and the Spirit of Capitalism* (New York: Penguin Books, 2002).

14. Michael Harrington, *The Other America* (New York: The Macmillan Company, 1962).

15. Ibid.

16. John P. Roche, *The Quest for the Dream* (New York: The Macmillan Company, 1963), 9.

17. Mark Twain and Charles D. Warner, *The Gilded Age* (London: Chatto & Windus, 1897).

18. Adams, *The Epic of America*, 415.

19. Martin Luther King Jr., "The American Dream," speech given February 5, 1964, at Drew University, Madison, New Jersey.

20. Malcolm X, "The Ballot or the Bullet," speech given April 3, 1964, in Cleveland, Ohio, in *Malcolm X Speaks: Selected Speeches and Statements*, George Breitman, ed. (New York: Grove Press, 1965), 26.

21. John M. Duncan, *Travels through part of the United States and Canada in 1818 and 1819*, vol. 2 (New York: W. B. Gilley, 1823), 338–339.

22. Mary McCarthy, "American Playwrights," *Encounter*, vol. 17 (1961), 28.

23. Henry Miller, *The Air Conditioned Nightmare* (New York: New Directions Publishing, 1945). Miller's persistent use of the word "we" certainly did not imply that he included himself among the vulgar pushing mob.

24. Isaac Rosenfeld, review of Henry Miller's *The Air Conditioned Nightmare, Partisan Review* vol. 13 no. 3 (1946).

25. John Kenneth Galbraith, *The Affluent Society* (New York: Mentor Books, 1958).

26. Robert Rector and Rachel Sheffield, "Air Conditioning, Cable TV, and an Xbox: What is Poverty in the United States Today?" The Heritage Foundation (July 19, 2011).

27. Lydia Warren, "Luxury 99 per cent of Americans can only dream of . . . Michael Moore's stunning waterfront mansion revealed," *The Daily Mail* (November 13, 2011).

28. Michael Moore interview on GritTV (March 2, 2011).

29. Malia Zimmerman, "Van Jones Rallies with Hawaii's Community Organizers for 'Economic Fairness, Justice'—and a State Bank," *Hawaii Reporter* (March 21, 2012). It is not immediately clear how big Mr. Jones' house is, whether it could be considered a McMansion, or how many flat screen TVs he owns.

30. Transcript of Obama's remarks in Muncie, Indiana, on April 12, 2008. Note that this speech was an attempt to "clarify" remarks he had made the day before at a fundraiser at which he characterized those who opposed him as people who "get bitter, [who] cling to guns or religion or antipathy to people who aren't like them."

31. Timothy Gutowski et al., "Environmental Life Style Analysis (ELSA)," IEEE International Symposium on Electronics and the Environment, San Francisco, May 19–20, 2008.

32. The following is adapted from the author's "Thanks for our abundance," *The Washington Times* (November 23, 2011).

33. Elyssa East, "A Moveable Feast," *The New York Times* (November 23, 2009).

34. Elizabeth Mendes, "Optimism About Future for Youth Reaches All-Time Low," *Gallup Politics* (May 2, 2011). The report noted that those in the highest income groups were the most pessimistic about the future.

35. Associated Press (November 23, 2010).

36. CBS News Poll, May 20–24, 2010.

37. CBS News Poll, December 17–22, 2009.

38. Corry Schiermeyer, "Faith in American Dream Sinking as U.S. Adults Become Split Over Whether or Not They Can Achieve It," IBOPE Zogby Poll (July 20, 2011).

39. Quotes collected from the Occupy website, Wearethe99percent.tumblr.com.

40. "Second Annual State of the American Dream Survey," Center for the Study of the American Dream (Cincinnati, OH: Xavier University, March 2011).

Chapter 8

1. J. Hector St. John de Crèvecoeur, *Letters from an American Farmer/ by J. Hector St. John de Crèvecoeur, reprinted from the original ed., with a prefatory note by W. P. Trent and introduction by Ludwig Lewisohn* (New York: Fox, Duffield, and Company, 1904), 54–55.

2. Bruce Bradley and Dennis Stanford, "The North Atlantic ice-edge corridor: a possible Palaeolithic route to the New World," *World Archaeology,* vol. 36 no. 4 (2004), 459–478.

3. R. Dinmore in *London Monthly Magazine* (July 1, 1806), 502.

4. Quoted in Laura G. Craig, *America, God's Melting Pot* (New York: Fleming H. Revell Company, 1913), 22. Dickinson was a proponent of Manifest Destiny and foresaw a North American confederation under U.S. leadership.

5. Cecil Woodham-Smith, *The Great Hunger* (London: Penguin Books, 1991).

6. Prussian Chancellor Otto von Bismarck attempted to restrict emigration in the 1860s to preserve Prussia's mobilization base for conscription, but it was not greatly effective.

7. Charles Francis Adams, *The works of John Adams, second President of the United States. With a life of the author, notes and illus. by his grandson Charles Francis Adams* (Boston: Little, Brown and Co., 1856), 596.

8. The Sharpshooter, "The Bullseye," *The Commercial West* (July 12, 1913), 9.

9. "The American Character," in *The Literary magazine, and American register for 1804*, vol. 2, Charles Brockden Brown, ed. (Philadelphia: J. Conrad & Co., 1804), 252–253. The same author believed there were limits to the mixing in America, particularly between the northern and southern states: "The Americans can possess no other national character than what our common ancestors might be supposed to have had immediately after the succeeding irruptions of the Saxons, Danes, Romans, and Normans; and, in all probability, never will, as there is no less a difference between the northern and southern states, than betwixt the Hebrides and the West Indies." 254.

10. Quoted in Max Lerner, *America as a Civilization* (New York: Simon & Schuster, 1957), 29.

11. Israel Zangwill, *The Melting Pot: Drama in Four Acts* (New York: Macmillan, 1909).

12. "New Zangwill Play Cheap and Tawdry," *The New York Times* (September 7, 1909), 9.

13. Quoted in Todd Gitlin, "Yes We Did. Overcome," *The Atlantic* (November 11, 2008).

14. Quoted in Thomas Herbert, *Theodore Roosevelt, Typical American: His Life and Work* (New York: L. H. Walter, 1919), 367–68.

15. Theodore Roosevelt, *Fear God and Take Your Own Part* (New York: George H. Doran Co., 1916), 362.

16. Harris Interactive poll, *E Pluribus Unum: A Study of Americans' Views of National Identity*, commissioned for the Bradley Project on American National Identity, June 2008.

17. Ibid.

18. "Second Annual State of the American Dream Survey," Center for the Study of the American Dream (Cincinnati, OH: Xavier University, March 2011).

19. John Fetto, "An All-American Melting Pot—Americans' attitudes about being American," *American Demographics* (July 1, 2001).

20. Cf. *Worcester v. Georgia,* 31 U.S. (6 Pet.) 515 (1832), which affirmed Cherokee sovereign rights against the state of Georgia. President Andrew Jackson was reputed to have said in response, "John Marshall has made his decision; now let him enforce it."

21. Cf. Samuel Huntington, *Who Are We?* (New York: Simon & Schuster, 2004).

22. Quoted in Helen Fox, "*When race breaks out": conversations about race and racism in college classrooms* (New York: Peter Lang Publishing, 2009), 32.

23. Census data from "Mexican Immigrants in the United States, 2008," Pew Hispanic Center (April 15, 2009).

24. The people of the U.S. Commonwealth of Puerto Rico have a better claim to the argument. The current residents, who are U.S. citizens, can trace their lineage to those who were living there when the island was liberated from Spain in 1898. Referenda in 1967, 1993, and 1998 showed no conclusive desire to seek independence from the United States, and in a November 2012 referendum 61% approved of seeking statehood, versus 5.5% who favored independence.

25. See the author's editorial "Stinko de Mayo," *The Washington Times* (May 7, 2010), from which this section was taken.

26. Robert Jensen, "The Anguish in the American Dream," *Jadaliyya* (June 25, 2011).

27. "Second Annual State of the American Dream Survey."

28. Ibid.

29. FBI Uniform Crime Reports, Hate Crime Statistics, 2010. Also Jonathan S. Tobin, "FBI Statistics Belie Islamophobia Hysteria," *Commentary* (November 20, 2011).

30. The following section is adapted from the author's "Obama panders to Islam (again)," *The Washington Times* (September 4, 2009).

31. "Obama's Islamic America," *The Washington Times* (August 12, 2010).

32. See generally "Muslim Americans: No Signs of Growth in Alienation or Support for Extremism," Pew Research Center (August 30, 2011). See also Hamilton Nolan, "Report: Muslims More American Than You," *The Gawker* (August 30, 2011).

33. "Muslim Americans: No Signs of Growth in Alienation or Support for Extremism," Pew Research Center (August 30, 2011).

34. Steve Bannister, "Proud to be Americans," *Alexandria Daily Town Talk* (July 5, 2002).

Chapter 9

1. Jay Rey, "American and Proud of It," *Buffalo News* (June 24, 2002).

2. John Doherty, "New Roots Beyond the Old Country," *Syracuse Post-Standard* (November 24, 2002).

3. U.S. Department of Commerce Economics and Statistics Administration, *Meeting 21st Century Demographic Data Needs—Implementing the American Community Survey. Report 9: Comparing Social Characteristics With Census 2000* (Washington, D.C., June 2004), 44.

4. Dvora Yanow, *Constructing "Race" and "Ethnicity" in America* (London: M. E. Sharpe, 2003), 193.

5. Mark Krikorian, "Sending a Message with the Census," *National Review Online* (March 8, 2010). Krikorian said his "initial impulse was simply to misidentify my race so as to throw a monkey wrench into the statistics; I had fun doing this on the personal-information form my college required every semester, where I was a Puerto Rican Muslim one semester, and a Samoan Buddhist the next." But he cautioned that "lying in this constitutionally mandated process is wrong." It is also illegal.

6. 1980 Census, "Ancestry of Population by State, Supplementary Report PC80-S1-10" (April 1983), Washington, D.C.: U.S. Census Bureau, 6.

7. Deborah Bulkeley, "American Is Ancestry for Many," *Deseret Morning News* (November 23, 2006).

8. Quoted in John Doherty, "New Roots Beyond the Old Country."

9. "1990 Census of Population, Detailed Ancestry Groups for States, Report 1990 CP-S-1-2," Washington, D.C.: U.S. Census Bureau, B-1.

10. Sandra Yin, "Shifting Identities," *American Demographics* (December 1, 2001).

11. Yin, "Shifting Identities," III–3.

12. *Census Atlas of the United States, Series CENSR-29* (Washington, D.C.: U.S. Census Bureau, 2007), 139.

13. Angela Brittingham, "Comparison of Data on Ancestry: Census 2000, C2SS, and 2005 ACS," Washington, D.C.: U.S. Census Bureau (January 7, 2008), 14–15.

14. John Besl, "Census Ancestry Changes Reflect Changing America," *InContext* (September–October 2002).

15. Brittingham, "Comparison of Data on Ancestry," 14–15.

16. Colin Woodard, "A Geography Lesson for the Tea Party," *Washington Monthly* (November/December 2011). See also his intriguing *American Nations: A History of the Eleven Rival Regional Cultures of North America* (New York: Viking, 2011). With respect to southern Populists, Huey Long is a notable exception.

17. Quoted in John McCormick, "Obama defends comments about bitterness in small towns," *The Chicago Tribune* (April 11, 2008).

18. Nate Silver, "Pennsylvania Prediction: Clinton to net 12 delegates, 120K popular votes," FiveThirtyEight.com (April 16, 2008).

19. The 2010 ACS one-year estimate has 11,988,836 in urban areas (4.5% of urbanites) and 7,987,039 in rural areas (9.6% of people in rural areas).

20. Data from 2000 census and 2010 ACS three-year survey.

21. Quoted in Doherty, "New Roots Beyond the Old Country." Brown added, "It's one of the few questions on the census that I don't think has a federal program attached to it."

22. Quoted in John Frank, "One nation, indescribable," *Roanoke Times* (July 4, 2002).

23. Ibid.

24. Ibid.

25. Ibid.

26. Thomas Ginsberg, "In Mexico, Pa., Americans Rule by the Numbers," *Philadelphia Inquirer* (July 4, 2002).

27. John Fetto, "An All-American Melting Pot—Americans' attitudes about being American," *American Demographics* (July 1, 2001).

28. Ibid. Among Asians, 33 percent identify their culture and traditions as quintessentially American.

29. Harris Interactive poll, *E Pluribus Unum: A Study of Americans' Views of National Identity*, commissioned for the Bradley Project on American National Identity, June 2008. Democrats (30%) and Independents (25%) are more than twice as likely as Republicans (12%) to say there is no single definition of what it means to be an American.

Chapter 10

1. Peter Manso and Michael McClure, "Brautigan's Wake," *Vanity Fair* (May 1985), 62–68, 112–116.

2. Barak Obama, State of the Union address, January 24, 2012, Washington, D.C.

3. "A Frenchman's View of It," *The Catholic World*, 23 no. 136 (July 1876), 455.

4. Frank Putnam, "What's the Matter with New England?" *New England Magazine* (November 1907), 279.

5. President Jimmy Carter's July 15, 1979, speech on the "crisis of confidence" among the American people became known as the "malaise speech," although he never actually used the word at the time.

6. Paul Kennedy, *The Rise and Fall of Great Powers* (New York: Random House, 1987).

7. The war in Afghanistan cost $443 billion from 2001 through 2011, compared to the American Recovery and Reinvestment Act, which

by 2010 had cost $814 billion. See Amy Bingham, "Afghanistan War by the Numbers: Lives Lost, Billions Spent," ABC News (May 1, 2012).

8. Robert Kagan, *The World America Made* (New York: Alfred A. Knopf, 2012).

9. Henry James, *The Notebooks of Henry James,* Francis Otto Matthiessen, and Kenneth Ballard Murdock, eds. (Chicago: University of Chicago Press, 1981), 207. For James, the personification of this barbaric rise was American art collector Isabella Stewart Gardner. Also quoted in Adam Gopnik, "Decline, Fall, Rinse, Repeat," *The New Yorker* (September 12, 2011), 40.

10. Jeffrey M. Jones, "Americans Most Confident in Military, Least in Congress," *Gallup Politics,* (June 23, 2011).

11. "Second Annual State of the American Dream Survey," Center for the Study of the American Dream (Cincinnati, Ohio: Xavier University, March 2011).

12. Harris Interactive poll, *E Pluribus Unum: A Study of Americans' Views of National Identity,* commissioned for the Bradley Project on American National Identity (June 2008).

13. "Growing Gap in Favorable Views of Federal, State Governments," Pew Research Center (April 26, 2012).

14. Francois VI, Duc de la Rochefoucault-Liancourt, *Travels through the United States of North America, the country of the Iroquois, and Upper Canada, in the years 1795, 1796, and 1797; with an authentic account of Lower Canada* (London: R. Phillips, 1799), 553. La Rochefoucault wrote, "It is even astonishing to see how disrespectfully the people carry themselves, in regard to the courts of justice. They appear at the bar, with their hats on their heads, talk, make a noise, smoke their pipes, and cry out against the sentences pronounced. This last piece of conduct is universal."

15. Isaac Weld, *Travels through the states of North America and the provinces of Upper and Lower Canada during the years 1795, 1796, and 1797,* vol. 1 (London: J. Stockdale, 1799), 108.

16. Gallup polls of January 10–14, 2001 and January 7–9, 2011, reported on ThePollingReport.com.

17. Ibid.

18. "New Low: 17% Say U.S. Government Has Consent of the Governed," Rasmussen Reports, (Sunday, August 07, 2011).

19. Quoted in "An American City That's Un-American," *The New York Times* (March 22, 1908).

20. The following is from the author's editorial "The Imperial District," *The Washington Times* (October 19, 2011).

21. Frank Bass and Timothy R. Homan, "Beltway Earnings Make U.S. Capital Richer Than Silicon Valley," Bloomberg.com (October 19, 2011).

22. Ibid.

23. Robert Pear, "Recession Officially Over, U.S. Incomes Kept Falling," *The New York Times* (October 9, 2011).

24. Catherine Rampell, "Washington, Capital of Economic Optimism," *The New York Times* (August 15, 2011).

25. Lydia Saad, "U.S. Political Ideology Stable With Conservatives Leading," *Gallup Politics* (August 1, 2011).

26. "Ideological News Sources: Who Watches and Why," The Pew Research Center (September 12, 2010).

27. On the Stewart/Fox controversy, see W. Gardner Selby, "Jon Stewart, Fox News & PolitiFact," Politifact.com (June 22, 2011). On June 21, Stewart said "I defer to [Politifact's] judgment and apologize for my mistake."

28. The author earned this title for arguing that George W. Bush deserved some credit for putting in place the systems that led to the Special Operations Forces' raid that took out Osama bin Laden in 2011. See "No Class—Obama Snubs Bush, Praises Himself on bin Laden Takedown," *The Robbins Report* (May 1, 2011).

29. Keith T. Poole, "The Decline and Rise of Party Polarization in Congress During the Twentieth Century," *Extensions* (Fall 2005), 5.

30. Google Ngrams data. For an early example, *Village Voice* columnist Jack Newfield said in 1968, "There may be no other way of saying that LBJ is simply not my president, the Democrats are not my party, and Vietnam

is not my war." Quoted in William F. Buckley, "Listen to the 'Voice,'" in his syndicated column of February 22, 1968.

31. Cf. the author's "Obama's Divided America," *The Washington Times* (February 1, 2012).

32. Lydia Saad, "Americans Express Historic Negativity Toward U.S. Government," *Gallup Politics* (September 26, 2011).

33. Lincoln to H. L. Pierce et al., April 6, 1859, in *Letters and Addresses of Abraham Lincoln*, Mary Maclean, ed. (New York: A. Wessels Co., 1907), 141.

34. Ronald Reagan, in a speech to the annual meeting of the Phoenix Chamber of Commerce, March 30, 1961.

35. Gary Schmitt and Cheryl Miller, "Why Is U.S. History High-Schoolers' Worst Subject?" *National Review Online* (June 16, 2011).

36. Alexander Heffner, "Former Supreme Court Justice Sandra Day O'Connor on the importance of civics education," *The Washington Post* (April 12, 2012).

37. John M. Duncan, *Travels through part of the United States and Canada in 1818 and 1819*, vol. 2, (New York: W. B. Gilley, 1823), 338–344.

INDEX

Page numbers followed by n indicate notes.